265.13   1-0314   c.1
Wag   Wagner, Johannes, ed.
            Adult Baptism and the Catechu-
        menate.

CONCILIUM

THEOLOGY IN THE AGE OF RENEWAL

CONCILIUM

CONCILIUM/VOL. 22

LITURGY

ADULT BAPTISM AND THE CATECHUMENATE

VOLUME 22

CONCILIUM
theology in the age of renewal

PAULIST PRESS
NEW YORK, N.Y. / GLEN ROCK, N.J.

Library of Congress Catalogue Card Number: 67-19979

Suggested Decimal Classification: 264.02

JACKET DESIGN: Emil Antonucci

Paulist Press assumes responsibility for the accuracy of the English translations in this Volume.

PAULIST PRESS
EXECUTIVE OFFICES: 304 W. 58th Street, New York, N.Y. and 21 Harristown Road, Glen Rock, N.J.
Executive Publisher: John A. Carr, C.S.P.
Executive Manager: Alvin A. Illig, C.S.P.
Asst. Executive Manager: Thomas E. Comber, C.S.P.

EDITORIAL OFFICES: 304 W. 58th Street, New York, N.Y.
Editor: Kevin A. Lynch, C.S.P.
Managing Editor: Urban P. Intondi

Printed and bound in the United States of America by
The Colonial Press Inc., Clinton, Mass.

CONTENTS

vii

PART II

BIBLIOGRAPHICAL SURVEY

Preface

After 350 years the shortcomings of the baptismal rite for adults in the Roman Ritual have generally been admitted. There is no better proof for this than the fact that in 1962, even before the start of the Council, the Congregation of Sacred Rites made a decision unheard of since the days of Paul V. It granted permission to divide the preparation for the adult rite of baptism, as set forth in the Roman Ritual, into seven stages. This was the first decisive step in a direction that both pastors and liturgists had been impatiently longing for, namely, the resacralization of the catechumenate, a problem which has since proved to be far more than merely a missionary problem. Its purpose was to aim at a purely rational outlook and to restore the originally intended functions of the various elements of the adult rite.

Future historians will praise the Congregation of Sacred Rites for having made an intelligent and carefully thought-out attempt at greater flexibility even before it had the backing of a Council. In spite of this it could not do in 1962 what had become possible in 1965 after the promulgation of the two Council documents on the liturgy and on the missions. These two documents not only grappled with the idea of dividing the solemn baptism of adults into stages, but they also ordered a general reform of this rite in the spirit of Article 66 of the *Constitution on the*

1

Sacred Liturgy. In this context the *Consilium ad exsequendam Constitutionem de S. Liturgia* (the body appointed to implement the Constitution) was able to release in 1965 a new rite for adults as an experimental guide for the bishops of the Consilium.

This volume of *Concilium,* therefore, falls between the beginning of this experiment and the establishment of the final rite, which, according to Article 39 of the Constitution, can only become a rite of the new Roman Ritual after being accepted for adaptation by the episcopal conferences. It is hoped that this volume may help to create that kind of theological climate which alone can make it possible for such far-reaching changes to succeed in the future of the Church. It deliberately refrains from dealing with the problems of infant baptism, not only because the preparatory work for reform is not yet sufficiently advanced, but also because in Article 67 the Council has decided on a revision of the rite for infant baptism which, for the first time in the history of our baptismal rite, will respect the *vera condicio infantium* (the factual condition of infants) in such a way that it will be a rite of its own and no longer practically identical with the adult rite as it still is today.

PART I
ARTICLES

Hendrik Manders, C.SS.R. / *Wittem, Netherlands*

The Relation between Baptism and Faith

To undertake a dialogue with the readers of *Concilium* is not as simple as it may appear. First of all, we should know about each other—where we stand on a subject, particularly when we speak of the relation between baptism and faith, which concerns the most fundamental principles of the doctrine on justification, of the sacraments, of God's appearance in this world, of Christian anthropology and many other problems. It makes a vast difference for purposes of discussion whether we begin with the question: "How do I find a merciful God?" (which looks on baptism as the sacrament of personal conversion, justification and sanctification), or whether we start with: "How does God appear in this world through baptism? How does he become again a living God in baptism?" (baptism as the manifestation of God). These questions of course are not mutually exclusive but imply each other, and yet how differently both faith and baptism operate according to which of these questions we begin with.

One steps into the baptismal water differently according to whether one thinks that faith uncovers the deepest meaning of human existence or whether one is convinced that in baptism we are dealing with divine realities. It makes a difference whether one thinks that grace is a purely immanent divine act and that, although it is a human reality, it is nevertheless essen-

4

tially invisible and accessible only to the faith, or whether one thinks that the incarnation of the Son of God implies essentially that grace becomes manifest in this world. To say that faith is only the condition or result of baptism is very different from saying that faith is achieved in baptism.

We could continue for a long time with this approach, and, in fact, we ought to so continue, because it is not merely a matter of facts and opinions. Theology is not merely an attempt to interpret scientifically the data of faith; it aims, at the same time, to make the authentic faith achievable in an authentic human way. Whatever opinion we may follow individually, within the Church we all have to go the same way. And while we all pursue the same way, it is important that we recognize each other as belonging to the same faith, and realize that whatever is being thought or said in theology, it all aims at preserving the heritage of the faith *intact,* which is not the same as *unchanged.* Therefore, it seems important to me that my readers and I can find a common starting point when we begin to reflect on the relation between faith and baptism, even though there is not much that is new. In fact, one might even think that in recent times enough has been said about all this and that we might well keep silent.[1] I hope that it is nevertheless possible to walk

---

[1] In what follows I should refer to many authors again and again, even if only as a token of gratitude for what I have received from them, but perhaps I may limit myself to the most important more recent publications I have been able to consult: H. F. Dondaine, "Le baptême est-il encore le 'sacrement de la foi'?" in *Maison Dieu* 6 (1946), pp. 76-87; M. Fraeyman, "Grondslagen van de innerlijke verhouding tussen geloof en doopsel," in *Coll. Gand.* (1947), pp. 166-80; P. T. Camelot, "Le baptême sacrement de la foi," in *Vie Spir.* 76 (1947), pp. 820-34; idem, *Spiritualité du baptême* (Paris, 1960); G. Geenen, "Fidei sacramentum," in *Bijdragen* 9 (1948), pp. 245-69; T. V. Baval, "Sacrament zonder geloof?" in *Bijdragen* 27 (1966), pp. 350-70; J. Hamer, "Le baptême et la foi," in *Irénikon* 23 (1950), pp. 387-405; R. Schnackenburg, *Das Heilsgeschehen bei der Taufe nach dem Apostel Paulus* (Munich, 1950), pp. 115-20, 185-95; E. Schillebeeckx, *De sacramentele heilseconomie* (Antwerp, 1952), pp. 557-663; idem, *Vers un catéchuménat des adultes.* Cahier spécial de la documentation catéchistique (Paris, 1957); P. Herbin, *Naissance du chrétien* (Paris, 1957); J. Goffinet, "Le baptême, sacrement de la foi," in *Rev. Eccl. Liège* 45 (1958), pp. 333-51; L. Bouyer, *L'initiation chrétienne* (Paris, 1958); N. Zeitsch.

together on a road that may lead to the understanding of a few more or less generally accepted conclusions that have been reached in recent years.

This relative unanimity leads curiously to the conclusion that baptismal practice *must* vary, both liturgically and pastorally.

I

THE FAITH THAT SEEKS GOD

Let us start with a point that is familiar to all of us: namely, that baptism is the sacrament of conversion and justification through faith.[2] This implies as a minimum that no one can be justified through baptism without believing. Faith is at least a condition for the reception of baptism and for receiving it sincerely.

Thus far, no one has any doubts concerning this definition.

Missionsw. 15 (1959), pp. 1-63 (number devoted to baptism); T. Ohm, *Das Katechumenat in den katholischen Missionen* (Münster, 1959); J. Lecuyer, "Théologie de l'initiation chrétienne chex les Pères," in *Maison Dieu* 58 (1959), pp. 5-26; P. Anciaux, *Het christendoopsel; leer, liturgie, zielzorg* (Malines, 1953); A. Stenzel, *Die Taufe* (Innsbruck, 1958); H. Wegman, "De zielzorg voor de dopelingen in de vasten en de paasweek," in *Tijds. Lit.* 44 (1960), pp. 134-44; L. Simons, "Naar een herstel van het katechumenaat," *ibid.*, pp. 145-53; R. Dijkers, "Christelijke initiatie in de missie," *ibid.*, pp. 154-65; H. Mentz, *Taufe und Kirche in ihren ursprünglichen Zusammenhang* (Munich, 1960); J. Delmotte, "Het doopsel, sacrament van het geloof," in *Coll. Brug. Gand.* 8 (1962), pp. 3-31; J. Duplacy, "Le salut par la foi et le baptême d'après le Nouveau Testament," in *Lum. et Vie* 27 (1956), pp. 3-52; T. Maertens, *Histoire pastorale du rituel du catéchuménat et du baptême* (Bruges, 1962); *idem*, "Catéchuménat et liturgie," in *Maison Dieu* 71 (1962); A. Turck, "Aux origines du catéchuménat," in *Rev. Sc. Phil. Théol.* 48 (1964), pp. 20-31; T. Halton, "Baptism as Illumination," in *Irish Theol. Quart.* 32 (1965), pp. 28-41; F. M. Braun, "Le don de Dieu et l'initiation chrétienne," in *NRT* 96 (1964); N. Hofer, "Das Bekenntnis 'Herr ist Jesus' und das 'Taufen auf den Namen des Herrn Jesus'," in *Tüb. Theol. Quart.* 145 (1965), pp. 1-12; H. B. Rossen, "Verbond en besnijdenis bij Paulus in verband met de doop," in *Ned. Theol. Tijds.* 19 (1965), p. 433; H. Pesch, "Umkehr, Glaube und Taufe," in *Bibel u. Leben* 7 (1966), pp. 1-14.

[2] Cf. *Conc. Trid.* Sess. VI, c.7 (DS 1529 [DB 799]).

That is precisely why it is useful to think a little further about this faith. What kind of faith is required as a condition for baptism, a way to justification? The Council of Trent describes this faith, this "beginning of justification",[3] perhaps not completely but in its essential outline, as a progressive self-awareness of man in his relation to God in the light of the Gospel and as a way that leads to baptism.[4] One might also say that this faith is described as a recognition of God as the one who, faithful to his promise, justifies the sinner gratuitously. This recognition is connected with the witness (kerygma) of the Church. One might also formulate this in a more modern sense and say that in this preliminary faith man discovers what it is to be "man". This faith uncovers for him the reality of his existence at its deepest level. In this way he discovers that to live means to be committed to conversion. What this conversion contains is too complex for the present discussion. But in any case it means that in the first place man turns toward a faithful and true God; in relation to this, particular dogmatic truths are relevant.[5] In modern parlance one might say that this contains a conversion to one's fellow man. In effect, how could one truly believe in Jesus Christ without one's fellow man? But I would like to add that because faith embraces conversion, it is not enough to say that this faith only gives a deeper insight into human reality. No doubt, it does give this insight into human reality, but it does so not merely to see it; it does so in order to make it real as the Gospel requires it to be.

This is important for our outlook on baptism. But it also implies some important conclusions insofar as the ecclesiastical preparation for baptism is concerned. The preliminary faith reaches us through "hearing". But this means at least that the Church—both the universal and the local Church—makes her

[3] *Ibid.*, c.8 (DS 1522 [DB 801]). I might point out that the term "faith" does not always mean the same thing in this Session of Trent.
[4] *Ibid.*, c.6 (DS 1526 [DB 798]).
[5] "Believing those things to be true that are divinely revealed and *promised, and above all that the sinner is justified by God through his grace. . . .*"

voice audible in the world in one way or another by word or deed, so that a confrontation with her preaching can take place. For some people, particularly in the cultural environment of the West where the press and other means of communication have such an extensive influence, it is possible to have knowledge of the Church's preaching through personal study, personal and informal contacts and personal practice. In this way, one acquires this preliminary faith without formal contact with the Church. But it would appear normal that the formation and development of this faith should come about under the influence and guidance of the actually proclaiming Church. And this is the foundation of the catechumenate.

History shows that this catechumenate can take various forms, not only insofar as the organization and plan are concerned, but also with regard to its "official" character. This may vary from the informal assistance of a layman—who then should be answerable for his candidate at baptism—to an official institution of, for example, a qualified group formed by the official representatives of the Church for the community. It may take a liturgical form or not. It is not possible to lay down norms that are universally valid. Rather, it would seem that every particular Church must make such decisions in its own way according to its own needs and those of the candidate.[6] Nevertheless, some general observations may be made.

From what has been said about the nature of this faith that precedes baptism, it follows that the formation of the candidate should not be primarily a matter of introducing him to the doctrinal faith of the Church, and certainly not to its full contents. This is clear from the fact that, at the time when it reached its highest peak, the official catechumenate put the initiation into the sacraments (baptism included) *after* baptism. Whether or not the catechumenate embraces a comprehensive doctrinal instruction will depend on the circumstances and on the Church's

---

[6] It is no doubt in this spirit that Art. 64 of the *Constitution on the Sacred Liturgy* will have to be applied. Note the place assigned here to the local Ordinary at this revision of the catechumenate.

practice. But what certainly must be accomplished during this period is the formation of the candidate in faith in "God who justifies the sinner". This means that the essential message of the Gospel about man, about Jesus Christ, about the Father and the Spirit of Christ, must be brought out in such a way that a genuine "conversion" can take place, a genuine belief in a God who is actually engaged in making himself true in Christ in this world through us. The candidate for baptism must be confronted with what scripture calls "the way". This obviously includes some doctrinal instruction, but this instruction must serve what should really take place in the candidate himself.

Insofar as the liturgical form is concerned, I would like to say that it is not easy to state how this should be done. Various parts of our present baptismal ritual might be very satisfactory in some cases. But one can easily think of circumstances where this ritual cannot be used, either because of the present form of the ritual [7] or because of the prayers. Thus the exorcisms seem to me very suitable in certain non-Western cultural milieux. In the West they seem to be impossible. It is simply a fact that the power of evil is experienced here in the West in a way that is very different from that expressed in the exorcisms. However this may be, every Church will have to give its own expression to its own catechumenate. And this expression will vary again according to whether it is a communal catechumenate or a personal one. The important thing is that, whatever the form, it should be realistic and meaningful.

Once a Church has introduced a liturgical form for its catechumenate, it must be maintained that this is part of the sacrament of baptism. The reason is that such an ecclesial form makes explicit an essential element of baptism in which justification by faith is in the process of being achieved in a ritual: i.e., in an ecclesially visible manner. This essential element is precisely the progressive building up of the faith that justifies, insofar as this

---

[7] For difficulties that may arise from such things as, for example, the unctions, cf. J. Beckmann, "Taufvorbereitung und Taufliturgie in den Missionen vom 16 Jahrhundert bis zur Gegenwart," in *N. Zeitschr. Missionsw.* 15 (1959), pp. 14-31.

implies a conversion to the living God and to Christ the Lord. The sacrament of baptism begins to unfold itself in the catechumenate and manifests itself there as the "sacrament of faith".

If we think for a moment about the faith as it appears at this stage, we shall see that it is seen in various functions that are intimately connected with each other. There is, first of all, the Church as the community which believes that God's promises are truly fulfilled in Christ, that the Church is the community to which is imparted the Spirit who makes these promises come true even now. For it is in confrontation *with* and under the guidance *of* this faith that is announced to him that the faith of the baptismal candidate comes to life and develops. It is important to note here that the Church must proclaim this certainty in the catechumenate: "He who believes [i.e., who confesses this certainty of the Church] and is baptized [i.e., who joins this community] is saved." But it is equally important that the baptismal candidate understand that this certainty also implies, for the Church, a constant seeking, and that he is initiated in the necessary "uncertainty" that is included in the certainty. At the moment this is surely not an easy task. But it is the more necessary as this uncertainty has come to the fore today. Otherwise this uncertainty would shock an unprepared person in that basic certainty which the Church must proclaim to him in faithfulness to the Lord.

When the faith of the baptismal candidate develops in intimate union with this faith of the Church, it means that we are not concerned here with the unfolding of one or another neutral, metaphysical experience of God through self-reflection, even though such an experience is not alien to his faith. It means that he assimilates in his personal conviction that faith of the community with which he is engaged in dialogue. As an attitude, his faith is certainly a personal faith. The meaning of this attitude, however, is determined by two factors: that in this attitude he takes part in the fulfillment of the Church's faith, and that through this participation he achieves contact with him in whom the Church believes, Jesus Christ, God's faithful witness. This point will be more fully treated below. At the moment it is important to see that already during this period of preparation the faith, of which baptism is the sacrament, is the faith of the Church.

II

THE FAITH THAT JUSTIFIES

A next step on which I think we can all agree might be described with the words of St. Basil: "The faith . . . is signified by baptism in water." [8] The way in which Trent describes the development of the preliminary faith, shows that it reaches its climax in the demand to be baptized. It is more or less the same in our present baptismal ritual, and one may say that it has always been so, although expressed in different ways. After the candidate has confessed his faith, the question is put to him whether he wants to be baptized: *Vis baptizari?* And when he has replied in the affirmative and by implication has asked for baptism, the sacrament is administered. It follows as a reply to his confession and his request. Thus, "I baptize you" sounds like a solemn confirmation by the Church of the confession made by the neophyte.[9]

His faith is sealed. What does this imply? First of all, it undoubtedly means that by baptizing him the Church accepts as authentic, and confirms, the candidate's confession and his request to join the Church which is implied in this (he says he believes "in the holy, Catholic Church"). This acceptance includes all the consequences: he is recognized as a member of the community where God's promises are fulfilled; his faith in the forgiveness of sins is valid for him personally; he enters into

---

[8] St. Basil, "De Spiritu Sancto" (I, 12), in *Patr. Gr.* 32, 117 (*Kai proagei men he homologia pros ten soterian eisagousa; epakoulouthei de to baptisma episphragizon emoon ten sugatathesin*).

[9] Cf. H. Manders, "Beschouwingen over sacramentele kernformules," in *Jaarboek W.K.T.N. 1960* (Hilversum, 1961), pp. 83-108, esp. pp. 104ff.

communion with God, with Christ his redeemer and Lord, and with the Spirit who brings about this redemption in the Church. His belief that God justifies the sinner is, so to speak, returned to him as valid for him personally.

So far there is no difficulty. In other words, in our liturgy we still apply the words we have all learned: namely, that the sacraments bring about the grace which they signify. But if we look closer into the baptismal ritual and the doctrine of justification, we shall have to take a further step and say that not only does baptism seal the faith of the neophyte, but that this faith is there fulfilled in the full sense of the word. Moreover, we shall have to say that the Church's message of salvation, and so her faith, is made real in the dialogue between the baptizer and the baptized. And here particularly we must maintain that the object of the faith, the mystery of Christ—or, if one prefers, the "Christ event"—becomes real in the attitude of faith and the proclamation, the kerygma. All this implies a whole complex of concrete, real factors of salvation. Only in this way do we have a more or less complete view of the function of faith in baptism. It would seem worthwhile to clarify this as far as possible, but this is not exactly a simple matter.

Perhaps the best thing is to begin with a quotation from Paul which describes tersely the various elements analyzed above and at the same time points beyond this: "The word [i.e., the word of *faith* which we preach] is near you, *on your lips* and *in your heart* because, if you confess with your lips that Jesus is Lord and believe in your heart that God raised him from the dead, you will be saved. For man believes with his heart and so is justified, and he confesses with his lips and so is saved" (Rom. 10, 8-10).

Here we see clearly, in a complementary parallelism,[10] that preaching, faith and confession form one whole in the act of justification. And this is precisely what I am concerned with here. One may take it as theological tradition in the Catholic

---

[10] According to the note in the Willibrord translation, attached to this text.

Church that God justifies man in the personal, free act of faith which he brings about in man through the Spirit, at least if we here understand by faith the full and free acceptance of the evangelical message as Paul sums it up in this text. If baptism is then truly the sacrament of justification, it means at least that in baptism the basic attitude of faith is given its definitive form.

But I think there is more to it. Not only does baptism bring about this basic attitude, but this attitude also becomes a full reality only then. In baptism the preliminary faith is given its really complete form, so that only then does it become real faith. This may sound peculiar, but this is how it appears to me.

What happens here? The preliminary faith gropes toward the full surrender to the Gospel's message. In dialogue with the preaching, it must discover what the fact of preaching in itself already says: justification and salvation are not limited to inner personal experiences. It is an essential feature of what happened in and through Christ that salvation and justification are public events. They are events that take place in full daylight because they take place in the Church. Ultimately this is so because justification is not only concerned with my personal salvation in view of an invisible hereafter, but also with the manifestation of God in this world. To be saved, to be justified, means, as the above text said, that Jesus is the Lord and that God has raised him from the dead. Justification is the manifestation of God's justice and mercy in the life of the Church. If this is so, it is an essential part of my faith that it be manifested as a public confession of this conviction. This is what takes place in baptism, as much to the faith of the neophyte as to that of the Church. The baptismal questions and answers are not merely a matter of information about the conditions required for a valid baptism. They both belong to the confession of the final stage and as such are already part of baptism. Only in this final joining up with the community that possesses the promises and the final reception by the community does the faith acquire its final shape, which is to witness to God's justice. And our justice consists precisely in its manifestation of God as a just God: i.e., a God who in Christ restores all things openly to their just proportions, to their original meaning.

And this leads to a whole series of further questions, which I can only touch upon. They begin with the question: Is all this not mere theological fiction? How can baptism show that God restores all things to their original meaning when in actual fact Christian communities and Christian individuals contribute to the destruction of this order? Does God really restore all things to their original intent in Christ? Doesn't this doctrine of justification through baptism lead to the creation of "puritans and pirates"?

Let us start by confessing that the belief that God raised Christ from the dead allows us to recognize that God makes the impossible possible in and through and in spite of the human condition. I am pleading here for an indestructible hope of the Christian that there will be a new earth, a hope which ought to be as deeply rooted and as dynamic in our conviction as a Marxist's hope is rooted in his.

But this is not the whole answer. We have to add that baptism means that the Christ-event takes place in the Church and in me. Baptism brings about in the Church what I believe: namely, that we are taken up into what God himself said must happen to the Lord at Jesus' baptism in the Jordan. If baptism means that through the faith we are incorporated in the paschal mystery, it nevertheless means this in a special way. We are baptized in the death and resurrection of Christ. But, as Mentz rightly pointed out, the believing entry into the water also means that we are baptized in order that in our own life we may share in the fulfillment of the Lord's life on earth in the light of his passion.[11] This means that each one's personal existence receives

---

[11] H. Mentz, *Taufe und Kirche in ihrem ursprünglichen Zusammenhang* (Munich, 1960), pp. 97f. That is why he calls baptism the "act of brotherhood". F. M. Braun, in "Le don de Dieu et l'initiation chrétienne," in *NRT* 96 (1964), pp. 1025-48, also shows that in the early Church baptism and the sacraments in general were seen as linked with the earthly life of the Lord. And this brings out the value and meaning of the *historical* existence of the Lord for the Church and for preaching.

its proper significance in baptism: to follow the way toward God in Christ through the vicissitudes of this life. And this, in turn, implies that we must live in such a way that God can become manifest to my brother as his Father. It means that, like the Lord, I must be concerned about my brother and committed to justice and peace. It means that the practice of my faith must show that even the apparently meaningless, the deglamorization of life and death itself have a meaning. The same holds for the community of the faithful as such. Thus the faith of baptism is an appeal. Thus it becomes possible for God to become manifest as the living God in the human existence within this world, but we must share in the responsibility for this. St. Thomas said: "Because water is transparent it can receive light: and so it is fitting that it should be used in baptism, inasmuch as it is the sacrament of faith." [12] Through the clearness of the water the light of the faith can reach us. It is this light by which we manifest God, "whoever or wherever he may be", to our brother in this world. How far we still are from the faith of our baptism!

[12] St. Thomas, *Summa theol.* III, q. 66, a. 3.

Louis Ligier, S.J. / *Rome, Italy*

The Biblical Symbolism of Baptism in the Fathers of the Church and the Liturgy

A complete typology of baptism would obviously go beyond the scope of a mere article; moreover, this is no longer required.[1] But it would seem opportune, both pastorally and theologically, to concentrate on the celebration of the baptismal liturgy for a better understanding of its symbolism. Such a rather limited study is in any case indispensable for any reflection on sacramental symbolism. I shall therefore start here with the unfolding of the celebration of baptism for adults, and try to explain the meaning of the rites and therefore of the sacrament in the light of scripture, the Fathers and the liturgical prayers.

There is no doubt that the baptismal liturgy has developed. Although today it is more complex than it was in the apostolic age, it is less so than it was between the 5th century and the Middle Ages. However, it has retained the dialogue, which expresses the step taken by the candidate, and has preserved the symbolic and sacramental rites: signs, unctions, exorcisms and the ritual of the water. Thus, in spite of the transformations, it still shows clearly the two dimensions of baptism as a sacramental act of the Church and a contribution to be made by man.

[1] The following studies may be useful: P. Lundberg, *La typologie baptismale dans l'ancienne Eglise* (Uppsala, 1942); J. Daniélou, *Sacramentum futuri. Etudes sur les origines de la typologie biblique* (Paris, 1950); *Bible et Liturgie*. Lex orandi, 11 (²1951).

This allows us to describe the symbolism of baptism as the rite of a covenant and as the sacrament of regeneration.

I

BAPTISM AS THE RITE OF A COVENANT

Do we realize that the commitments undertaken by the catechumen—the renunciation of Satan and the profession of faith—are both emphasized in the liturgy? They appear twice: at the beginning of the liturgy of the catechumens and at the most important moment immediately before the ritual of the water. This fact is evident since the 10th century in the Sacramentary of Fulda and generalized during the 16th century by the Roman Ritual of Gregory XIII. But as far back as the 3rd century both these gestures were made in Africa, in Carthage and perhaps also in Alexandria. Tertullian indeed points out that the catechumen "renounces the idols twice",[2] once "under the hand of the bishop".[3] And it seems that a page of Origen's *Exhortation to Martyrdom* must also be interpreted in the sense of a first abjuration "at the beginning of the catechumenate"[4] and a proper renunciation "at the moment of the covenant with God": i.e., at the moment of baptism.[5] Therefore, it is possible that the Roman ritual of Gregory XIII simply returned to an ancient practice. However true this may be, the effect of the repetition is that man's contribution becomes more important and its full meaning is brought out.

The Fathers of the 3rd, 4th and 5th centuries indeed saw a covenant with God in the renunciation of Satan and the profession of faith.[6] The liturgical expression may vary. In the

[2] Tertullian, *De Spectaculis* XIII, 1 (Corp. Christ. Ser. Lat. I), p. 239.

[3] *Idem, De corona* III, 2 (*ibid.*, II), p. 1024.

[4] Origen, *Exhortatio ad Martyrium* 17 (*P.G.* 11, 584c).

[5] *Ibid.*, 585a.

[6] *Idem, loc. cit.; In Numeros* hom. XII, 4 (*P.G.* 12, 665-66 = Sources chrét. 29, pp. 255-56); Cyril of Jerusalem, *Catechesis* III (*P.G.* 33, 425-28); Gregory of Nazianzus, *Oratio* XL, 8 (*P.G.* 36, 368); Didymus of

West the triple profession of faith by itself showed sufficiently the positive acceptance of Christ. In the East they insisted on a formula that formally balanced this positive engagement with the negative engagement of breaking with the devil. Thus, at Antioch the catechumen turned first to the West and said: "I detach myself from you, Satan, from your pomp, your worship and your angels." He then turned toward the East and added: "And I attach myself to you, O Christ." [7] However, these differences were of minor importance. St. Jerome had no objection to expressing himself by using the Eastern liturgy of Jerusalem.[8] In order to make his catechumens at Antioch realize the importance of their action, John Chrysostom explained it to them in simple language reminiscent of St. Paul: "We have all signed a treaty with Christ, not with ink but with the spirit, nor with the pen but with our word. . . . We have confessed the sovereignty of God and repudiated the tyranny of the devil. There you have the signature, the agreement, the contract." [9] Every Christian understood that he had to keep this commitment constantly in mind.

Compared with the Old Testament, the questions implied in this "agreement" showed some new features: the spontaneity of the catechumen, the individual approach and occasionally, somewhere in the background, the idea of a pact with Satan. But these new features should be understood within the context of

---

Alexandria, De Trinitate II, 13 (P.G. 39, 689-91); John Chrysostom, Huit Catéchèses baptismales inédites II, 21-22 (=Sources chrét. 50, A. Wenger, p. 145); III, 20; III, 162-63; IV, 31-32; IV, 198-99; Theodore of Mopsuestia, Les Homélies catéchétiques XII, 26-27 (=Studi e Testi, p. 145; R. Tonneau and R. Devreesse, pp. 363-65); XIII, 4 (ibid., p. 373); Tertullian, De Pudicitia IX, 16 (Corp. Christ Ser. Lat. II, 1298); Jerome, In Amos VI, 13 (P.L. 25, 1068); Augustine, Sermo 226 "Ad competentes," II, 2 (P.L. 38, 1077); Caesarius of Arles, Sermo XII, 4 (Corp. Christ. Ser. Lat. CIII, 60-61).

[7] John Chrysostom, Ad Colossenses, hom. VI (P.G. 62, 342). A. Wenger has collected the various formulae used by Chrysostom in his Introduction to the Huit catéchèses baptismales inédites (Sources chrét. 50, pp. 81-82).

[8] Loc. cit. (P.L. 25, 1068).

[9] Huit catéchèses baptismales inédites II, 20 (Sources chrét. 50, pp. 162-63).

the theology of the covenant. One does not deny that the first initiative is God's; the catechumens are questioned as God questions them through the words of the Church. St. Augustine told them this in so many words: "It is a pact that God initiates with you." [10] And if, in contrast with the Old Testament, each one gives his personal answer, the reason is that this belonging to the People of God is no longer based on the flesh but on a personal faith. In any case it is a matter of belonging to the People of God: by leaving the followers of Satan the catechumen ranges himself with the disciples of Christ. The communal dimension of the "agreement" is evident.

Equally clear is the continuity of this agreement or covenant, particularly in the dialogue between celebrant and catechumen. Everything there reminds one of the renewals of this covenant (Gen. 35, 1-2; Deut. 27, 4-26), and particularly, as Origen had already observed,[10a] the celebration of Joshua 24. In the days of the patriarchs Joshua's homily, which recalls God's intervention in favor of his people, was a confession of faith. It was followed by interrogations that expressed the basic demand of the covenant: either to serve the one and only God exclusively or to choose some other pseudo-god. Israel loudly proclaimed its loyalty, and Joshua demanded a practical conclusion: they had to strive to eliminate alien gods and adhere with their whole heart to the God of their fathers. All this followed a liturgical rhythm: exhortation, dialogue and proclamation of their adhesion to the true God and of their breaking with all false gods.

It is well known that this pattern of celebrating the renewal of the covenant, based on and developed in a theology of the Word, inspired the preaching to the proselytes and the Qumran literature of the "new covenant" in the days of Christ. This catechesis, organized on the theme of the "two ways", ended with an initiation rite. The apostles followed the same line for their preaching and no doubt for their liturgy. Romans 10, 6-8 repeats the adjuration contained in Deuteronomy 30, 11-14. In several epistles the exhortations are built up on a pattern of

[10] *Sermo* 226 "*Ad competentes*," II, 2 (*P.L.* 38, 1077).
[10a] Cf. *supra*, footnotes 4 and 5.

repudiation and adhesion,[11] and the discourses in the Acts of the Apostles speak in terms of option and transition: from darkness to light, from the kingdom of Satan to that of God.[12] The baptismal rite then fits naturally into a liturgy of the covenant.

But in the Old Testament the covenant was spoken of in terms of a nuptial alliance. The covenant of the desert was the "engagement" between God and Israel. For Cyril of Jerusalem, John Chrysostom and Cyril of Alexandria, too, the catechumens' pact with Christ was a nuptial contract. Their engagement is not merely the commitment of a soldier who enrolls, as suggested by the vocabulary in use at Antioch of an *apotaxis* (a setting apart) and a *syntaxis* (a joining),[13] for even at Antioch Chrysostom used the nuptial psalm 45 (44) when commenting on the renunciation. He explained the "renounce Satan" as the messianic invitation to the bride: "Hear, my daughter . . . forget your people and the home of your father." [14] Cyril did the same at Alexandria.[15] The baptismal pact is a prelude to the mystical marriage. Therefore, Chrysostom opened his baptismal homilies with this theme.

This nuptial conception of the covenant had a practical aspect. Granted that the contract and the bath were part of the Semitic marriage ritual, the initiation liturgy could, by means of this nuptial symbolism, quite naturally pass from the commitment to the baptismal rite. This is, in fact, suggested by St. Paul in the noble text of Ephesians 5, 25-27, where the meaning slides from the cleansing of the Church by the Bridegroom into the "washing of water with the Word" that sanctifies the Christian—that is, baptism. Chrysostom's reference to it was therefore most fitting. The nuptial interpretation of the alliance thus

[11] Gal 5, 16-25: the opposition between spirit and flesh. Eph. 4, 22: one must relinquish one's former kind of life and put off one's old nature; Eph. 4, 24: one must put on the new man; Eph. 5, 2: one must follow the way of love in imitation of Christ; Eph. 6, 11: one must put on the armor of God. Cf. Col. 3, 8ff.

[12] Acts 14, 15; 26, 18.

[13] *Constitutiones Apostolorum* VII, 41, 1-2 (ed. Funk I, pp. 444-45). Cf. *supra*, footnote 7.

[14] *Huit catéchèses* . . . I, 9-10 (*loc. cit.*, pp. 112-13).

[15] *In Psalmum XLIV* (*P.G.* 69, 1043-44).

enabled the baptismal liturgy to link the ritual of the pact with that of the immersion.

In any case, this was its role in the liturgies of Syria and Antioch. From the blessing of the font onward, the theme of motherhood is insisted upon: the font is a "maternal womb"; like the Church, it is given the noble name of "mother of life".[16] The neophytes are congratulated on being "sons of the Church and of baptism".[17] But at the beginning of this liturgy the Church is called the Bride. The hymns show her wandering by the banks of the Jordan, looking for the Bridegroom who is hidden and will be revealed to her by John the Baptist: "Near the Jordan I was seized with astonishment and I saw something marvelous when the glorious Bridegroom showed himself preparing the wedding of the Bride and her sanctification. . . . The beauty of the Bride was dazzling but she still did not know who was the Bridegroom she expected. . . . Then the Bridegroom showed himself and descended into the river near John." [18]

But from the biblical point of view the "new alliance", of which baptism is the sacrament, cannot be reduced to a simple renewal of the covenant according to the old rite. Hence, the baptismal liturgy was complemented in various ways which have to be taken into account: exorcism and unction.

The new covenant is marked by an "eschatological crisis". Jesus' preaching took place between his temptation and the darkness of his passion. It was a period of opposition, formerly hidden but now in the open, between Christ and the devil. In this context the evangelical option for the faith took on an element of risk and deliverance. It seems that the baptismal exorcisms correspond to the reality of this evangelical context. Indeed, it is not enough for the liturgy to confer the riches of adoption, but it must also bring out the price paid for it by giving expression to the eschatological tension that had marked its origin. The exorcisms are therefore necessary in order to

[16] *Ordo baptismi*, attributed to Severus of Antioch in J. Assemani, *Codex liturgicus Ecclesiae universalis* II (Paris, ²1902), p. 286.

[17] *Ibid.*, p. 344.

[18] *Ibid.*, I, p. 241.

bring to the rite of the covenant, beyond the terse juridical character of its dialogue, the evangelical truth of the hour that it re-creates: the passage from darkness to the kingdom of God, from servitude to freedom.

By the same token, the covenant rite is given its human truth. In effect, the catechumen discovers a new universe in the faith, but not without some real apprehension. The last exorcism assures him of the Church's support. The Coptic liturgy makes him go down on his knees at this moment, and reminds him of the strength he will receive from him who has been given a name above all names and before whom every knee bends, even in hell.[19] He will be a victor forever, but on his knees.

Insofar as the unction is concerned, which for a long time used to be conferred without any other formula but that of the exorcism,[20] it was first linked up with the renunciation and the exorcism. Originally, it was known by the latter name. It fortifies the catechumen against temptation: "The enemy does not dare look a person in the face when he sees there the brilliant light of this unction which blinds him." [21] The symbolism, therefore, is that of the unction of the disciples sent on their evangelical mission[22] or of the priest who purifies the leper.[23]

But the unction acquired an additional value which underlines its evangelical meaning. The Latin liturgy was not satisfied with the formula of the apostolic tradition but introduced another one which anticipated the theme of the post-baptismal unction: "I anoint you . . . in Christ Jesus our Lord for . . . eternal life." The meaning had become positive. At Jerusalem

---

[19] Phil. 2, 9-10; J. Assemani, op. cit., I, p. 161; H. Denzinger, Ritus Orientalium I (Graz, ²1961), p. 199.

[20] Thus in the baptismal Orders X, XI, and XII in Martène, De antiquis Ecclesiae ritibus I, c. I, XVIII (Antwerp, 1763), pp. 70-72. Cf. B. Botte, La Tradition apostolique de saint Hippolyte 21 (Münster i. Westf., 1963), p. 46.

[21] John Chrysostom, op. cit. supra, footnote 6, II, 23 (Sources chrét., pp. 146-47).

[22] Mk. 6, 13; cf. Jas. 5, 14; cf. the Euchologion of Serapion XXII in Funk, Didascalia et Constitutiones Apostolorum II (Paderborn, 1905), pp. 184-85.

[23] Lev. 14, 17-18; J. Assemani, op. cit., II, p. 241; Denzinger, op. cit., I, p. 224.

Cyril went further and maintained that this first unction showed that the catechumen "has been taken from the wild olive tree and grafted on to the good one so that he has begun to share in the fruitfulness of the true olive tree".[24] In this way it fits the evangelical moment of conversion and the two aspects of the covenant rite: it severs and it unites. Once clearly expressed by Cyril, this symbolism entered into the liturgical formulae of Syria and Egypt: "N. . . has been marked with the oil of gladness against all activity of the adversary and is grafted on the good olive tree of the holy, catholic and apostolic Church in the name of the Father and the Son and the Holy Spirit." [25]

II

BAPTISM, THE SACRAMENT OF REGENERATION

The covenant rite, however, although it expresses so well the faith and the will to enter the Church, does not constitute the sacrament. However important it may be in the liturgy for adults, it is less important than the rite of the water which was for a long time—and in the East still is—total or partial immersion.

This rite had a natural meaning that preceded it. The washing and physical restoration of the body by bathing symbolize purification, the remission of sins and the renewal of the spirit. But once Jesus had chosen it to be the initiation sacrament for his disciples, he endowed it with a new symbolism.

[24] *Mystagogical Catechesis* II, 3 (*P.G.* 33, 1080A).

[25] J. Assemani, *op. cit.,* I, pp. 240, 254-55; H. Denzinger, *op. cit.,* I, pp. 273, 284. In Egypt the formula is significant: "I anoint you with the oil of gladness" (J. Assemani, *op. cit.,* I, p. 163; Denzinger, *op. cit.,* I, p. 200). On the other hand, the Byzantine liturgy has kept the primitive Eastern formula unadorned: "The servant of God, *N,* is anointed with the oil of gladness in the name of the Father and the Son and the Holy Spirit now and always and forevermore" (J. Goar, *Euchologion sive Rituale Graecorum* [Venice, ²1730], p. 290). The Maronites enriched it but, following Theodore of Mopsuestia (*Hom. XIII,* 17), they only mention the positive aspect, the admittance to Christ's flock: "*N,* now to be baptized, is signed as a lamb in the flock of Christ, in the name of the Father and the Son and the Holy Spirit" (J. Assemani, *op. cit.,* II, p. 316; H. Denzinger, *op. cit.,* I, p. 341).

In relation to Christ it was understood first as a mystical identification with his passion and resurrection. This was the teaching
of St. Paul. Jesus had inaugurated this symbolism by announcing his own death in terms of a baptism[26] and by asking his
followers to take up their cross and to follow him. The Fathers,
who were so attached to this identification of the Christian with
Christ, retained it. As St. Ambrose put it: "You have been
bathed, and thereby you have been buried with Christ. . . . It
is, therefore, a death, not in bodily reality but symbolically.
When, therefore, you have been bathed, you take on the like-
ness of his death and his burial." [27] In the East Narsai summed
it up in these general terms: "Death and life: that is the mystery
of baptism." [28] The rite showed this by itself: it was enough to
see the neophyte disappear into the font where he had been
placed. The catechetist had only to comment. At Jerusalem, in
the basilica of the Anastasis not far from the holy sepulchre, he
recalled the three days that Jesus lay in the tomb, and which
he saw symbolically in the triple immersion.[29] In a more general
way the Fathers stressed the two essential moments, immersion
and emersion. At Antioch Theodore of Mopsuestia explained:
"When at my baptism I put my head under water I received
the death of our Lord, the Christ, and wish to take on me his
burial; and thereby I truly confess the resurrection of our Lord.
But when I come out of the water I believe I am already
resuscitated in a symbolic fashion." [30] It is easy to see that this
symbolism is particularly suited to show the fruits of the
paschal mystery which have been communicated through baptism: forgiveness of sins and victory over death and corruption.
By the same token it is essentially christological.

This christological orientation was not affected by the trinitarian interrogations that for a long time accompanied the triple

[26] Lk. 12, 50.
[27] *De Sacramentis* II, 20, 23 (Sources chrét. 25*bis*, pp. 86-88).
[28] Homily XXII, in A. Mingana, *Narsai Doctoris Syri Homiliae et
Carmina* I (Mosul, 1905), p. 364 (Eng. tr: R. Connolly in *Texts and
Studies* VIII/1, 1909, p. 41).
[29] Cyril of Jerusalem, *Myst. Catech.* II, 4 (*P.G.* 33, 1080C).
[30] Homily XIV, 5, *op. cit.* (*supra*, footnote 6), p. 413.

immersion. They joined the rite of the water with the covenant in order to show that baptism was the sacrament of faith. In contrast, the use of two baptismal formulae,[31] traditional in the East, gave the christological symbolism a trinitarian slant and prepared, insofar as the liturgy is concerned, the complementary symbolism of regeneration. Indeed, having been baptized by the Church in the name of the Persons invoked on him, the neophyte was not only assimilated to Christ but also adopted by the Trinity and received by the Church. He had joined the community of the sons of God.[32]

This led to the complementary symbolism of regeneration. The previous symbolism, based on the mystery of Christ's death and resurrection, took the catechumen through the central meaning of history. It made him belong no longer to the first Adam; it grafted him on the new Man and so made him a new creature. The symbolism of regeneration, on the contrary, points directly toward heaven, is vertical and centered on God. It confers filial adoption in the name of the Trinity. Moreover, it is based on Christ's formal teaching: "Unless one is born of water and the Spirit, he cannot enter the kingdom of God." [33] Therefore, baptism is a birth, a new birth, as Nicodemus saw at once. And Paul's letter to Titus consequently calls it "the bath of regeneration".[34]

The Fathers and the Eastern liturgies developed and deepened this basic symbolism. According to Pseudo-Dionysius, the baptistry is the "mother of filial adoption".[35] The baptismal water is a "maternal womb" [36] and the neophyte is "a son born of

[31] As is known, the two baptismal formulae, "I baptize you . . ." and "*N* is baptized", both come from the East. Cf. E. Whitaker, "The History of the Baptismal Formula," in *Journ. Eccl. Hist.* 16 (1965), pp. 1-12.

[32] As Ambrose wrote in his *De Sacramentis,* regeneration and resurrection are one and the same. "When the Son rose from the dead, the voice of the Father was heard: 'You are my Son; today I have begotten you.' The regeneration from the baptismal water is therefore also a resurrection" III, 2 (Sources chrét., 25*bis,* p. 90).

[33] Jn. 3, 5.

[34] Tit. 3, 5.

[35] *He meter tes uiothesias,* in Pseudo-Dionysius, *Hier. Eccl.* II, 7 (*P.G.* 3, 396C).

[36] Ephrem, *De Virginitate* VII, 7-8 (Corp. Script. Christ. Orient., Ser.

water in the name of the Trinity".[37] When he steps out of the water, "everybody embraces him and kisses him as a newly-born child".[38] These metaphors, which express the Church's maternal feelings, should not mislead us. A Syro-Antioch baptismal order links it theologically with the eternal generation of the Son: "The Word of God, born impassibly and ineffably of the Father . . . bestowed on mankind the new birth of water and the Spirit, the luminous robe of baptism, the supreme gift of adoption and kinship with the Father and the Spirit." [39] Incarnation has reached its aim: in his firstborn Son, the Father has taken unto himself adopted sons.

Because of its importance, this symbolism was given a new and unexpected place in the liturgy: namely, in the blessing of the baptismal water. Since, indeed, it is not only a question of being reborn but really of being born "from on-high", water alone is not enough and the Spirit must be involved.[40] At the end of the 2nd century the liturgical blessing of the baptismal water had already eliminated all dualism and shown that there is but one baptism of water and the Spirit, as Christ wanted it. The Fathers in no way underrated the natural dignity and value of the water,[41] but, as Tertullian said: "It only plays a part in the mystery of our sanctification once God has been invoked over it." [42] This soon became common practice as Origen frequently emphasized.[43] The power of the baptismal water is attributed to the working of the Spirit and the epiclesis of the

---

Syr., 95, pp. 26-27); Narsai, *op. cit.*, Hom. XXII, in A. Mingana, *op. cit.*, p. 358 (Eng. tr.: R. Connolly, *op. cit.*, p. 34).

[37] *Brevis Ordo Baptismi*, attributed to Severus of Antioch, in J. Assemani, *op. cit.* II, p. 300; cf. H. Denzinger, *op. cit.*, I, p. 308.

[38] Narsai, *Homily XXI*, in A. Mingana, *op. cit.*, p. 346; Eng. tr.: R. Connolly, *op. cit.*, p. 52.

[39] *Ordo baptismi pro pluribus*, in J. Assemani, *op. cit.*, II, pp. 254-55; H. Denzinger, *op. cit.*, I, pp. 298-99.

[40] Jn. 3, 3: *anôthen*.

[41] According to Tertullian, it has even "merited its sacramental function" (*De Baptismo* III, 1, ed. Sources chrét. 35, p. 67).

[42] *Ibid.*, IV, 4 (Sources chrét. 35, p. 70).

[43] Cf. W. de Vries, *Sakramententheologie bei den Nestorianern* (Rome, 1947), p. 170.

three Persons. "The water does not purify without the Spirit." [44]
"The pontiff uses consecrated formulae and blessings; he asks
that the grace of the Spirit may come down on the water and
make it perfect in view of all this." [45]

This explains the magnificent consecratory prayers linked with
the baptismal rite since the 4th and 5th centuries. Following the
style of the eucharistic prayer, they forcibly express the symbolism of the water and underline the effects of baptism better than
any other part of the liturgy. They sum up the patristic catechesis of baptism. The Coptic liturgy has preserved a fine sample
of this.[46] The first part describes in grand style the role of water
in the divine economy: the creation of the earth out of the
waters, the gathering and containing of the waters in the name
of the Lord, God's victory over the infernal monster on the
waters and God's saving power manifested through the waters
even in the unleashing of the deluge. The *anamnesis* pursues
this in greater detail. It shows how God is feared by the waters
of the abyss. Through Moses God divided the waters in order
to create a passage for the Israelites and to baptize them through
his intervention. Through Joshua he again triumphed over the
waters. In the days of Elijah he announced the rebirth through
baptism and cured Naaman in the Jordan. At this point the
commemoration finishes with these words of the Gospel: "For
you are all-powerful and with you nothing is impossible." Then
begins the *epiclesis:* "Show yourself; look upon this water, your
creature; bestow on it the grace of the Jordan, the virtue and
power of heaven; and through the descent of the Holy Spirit
grant it the blessing of the Jordan. Give it the power to be the
water that vivifies, sanctifies and purifies from sin, to be the
water of regeneration and of filial adoption." The water will no
longer bring death, but life.

There remains the last symbolism: the anointing that assimi-

---

[44] Ambrose, *De Mysteriis* IV, 19 (Sources chrét. 25*bis*, pp. 164-65).
[45] Theodore of Mopsuestia, *Homily* XIV, 10; *op. cit.*, p. 425.
[46] J. Assemani, *op. cit.*, II, pp. 170-173; H. Denzinger, *op. cit.*, I, pp.
205-06. A shorter text appears in A. Baumstark, "Eine aegyptische
Mess und Taufliturgie vermutlich des 6. Jahrhunderts," in *Oriens Chris-
tianus* I (1901), pp. 38-41.

lates the neophyte to Christ, causes him to partake of the anointing of the kings, prophets and priests of the Old Testament, and makes him a member of the royal and priestly people. This theme links up with the theme of the Christian as an "anointed" one.[47] From the dogmatic point of view, both ideas are ancient and common to East and West.

From the liturgical point of view, there is some variety. In the West it is linked with a tradition that can be traced from Tertullian via Ambrose, Augustine and Maximus of Turin to the Middle Ages and links the priestly dignity with the post-baptismal unction.[48] The East shows two rather different interpretations. Cyril of Jerusalem referred the symbolism to the anointing at confirmation,[49] where it was also found in Nicholas Cabasilas,[50] Simeon of Thessalonica[51] and probably in Germanus of Constantinople.[52] In the liturgical and theological tradition of Syria it was, since St. Ephrem,[53] linked with the prebaptismal unction of the catechumens, an interpretation found outside Syria in Hesychius of Jerusalem[54] and even in Nicholas Cabasilas, who brings the two Eastern traditions together.[55] In brief, the liturgical use of this theme is as wide as it is different.

[47] It is already found in Theophilus of Antioch in his letter to Autolycos, I, 12 (Sources chrét. 20, p. 85).

[48] Tertullian, *De Baptismo* VII, 1-2 (Sources chrét. 35, p. 76); Ambrose, *De Mysteriis* VI, 30 (Sources chrét. 25*bis*, pp. 172-73); Augustine, *De Trinitate* XV, 26, 46 (*P.L.* 42, 1093); Maximus of Turin, *De Baptismo* (*P.L.* 57, 778-79); Leidradus, *Liber de sacramento Baptismi* VII (*P.L.* 99, 863-65).

[49] *Myst. Catech.* III, 1, 6 (*P.G.* 33, 1088-89A, 1093A).

[50] *De vita in Christo,* lib. III (*P.G.* 150, 569AB and 580C).

[51] *De Sacramentis,* ch. XLIII (*P.G.* 155, 185D-188C); ch. LXXIII (*ibid.,* 244-45). This concerns the unction given after baptism, and therefore the one of confirmation according to his liturgy (248A).

[52] *Rerum Eccl. contemplatio* (*P.G.* 98, 385C-388C).

[53] *Hymni de oleo et oliva* XXVII, 5: "Oil, connected with the priesthood, *prepares the way* for baptism, like John, the priest's son" (Lamy, II, p. 802).

[54] *In Leviticum,* lib. II; *In Lev.* 8, 14-7 (*P.G.* 93, 880B); *In Lev.* 14, 18 (*ibid.,* 956D).

[55] *De vita in Christo,* lib. II (*P.G.* 150, 529CD). He is clearly inspired here by the formula used for the anointing of the catechumens: "The servant of God, *N,* is anointed with the *oil of gladness* . . ." because he refers directly to Ps. 44 (45), 8: "God, your God, has anointed you with the *oil of gladness.*"

Where do these differences come from? The laconic character of the formulae of anointing may have been the occasion of these differences but not the cause. We must look for other reasons. The position of the Byzantine theologians may have been inspired by their confirmation formula, which sees this unction as a "seal", and by the importance of the chrism as interpreted by Cyril of Jerusalem and developed in the consecratory prayers. This same reason is also valid for the Latin tradition, but in another sense.

What about the Syro-Antioch tradition? Does it intend to emphasize the commitments of baptism by attributing to the anointing of the catechumens beforehand the name and importance of the "oil of gladness"? Does it want to bring out more particularly the nuptial aspect of these commitments mentioned above, or perhaps their priestly value, as Origen suggested? [56] Or does this emphasis on the anointing of the catechumens reflect a Judaeo-Christian tradition which in this way replaced circumcision in the initiation of the proselytes? [57] Or, finally, could it simply reflect the hesitation of the Eastern Churches with regard to the essential rite of confirmation? The truth is that we do not know.

It is certain that in one way or another the Fathers and the various liturgies, not satisfied with reminding the neophytes of their share in Christ's priestly anointing, wanted to remind them

[56] His witness is important because his journeys and his stay at Caesarea allowed him to get acquainted with the Syrian liturgy, and the influence of his writings extended well beyond Egypt. In his commentary on Leviticus he observes that to renounce all and to attach oneself to Christ is a priestly act, a holocaust (In Lev., Hom. IX, 9; P.G. 12, 521CD). And this is what the catechumen does when he commits himself in baptism.

[57] At the initiation of the proselytes, circumcision preceded baptism. The unction of the catechumens may therefore well have appeared as a spiritualization of the "seal" of circumcision. Precisely at this unction of the catechumens the Syriac baptismal rite has a hymn that recalls the circumcision: "Among the nations he had set apart a people through the seal of circumcision. Now he has set apart the nations from the people through the seal of the anointing. For at the time when the nations wandered, he separated the people from them; and now that the people has lost its way, he has separated the nations from it" (J. Assemani, loc. cit., II, p. 241; H. Denzinger, loc. cit., I, p. 294).

also of their share in the anointing of the prophets, kings and priests. The economy of the People of God continues and broadens from the Old Testament to the New. This is a common theological theme and, although influenced by the rite of confirmation, it is primarily baptismal. This was the understanding of Syro-Antioch liturgy, for when the catechumen was going to step into the piscina, his whole body was anointed. The celebrant then pronounced the words of the messianic and nuptial psalm: "Therefore God, your God, has anointed you with the oil of gladness above your fellows; your robes are all fragrant with myrrh and aloes." [58] At the same time, the deacons sang the following hymn: "God said to Moses that he should anoint Aaron with holy oil in order to consecrate him; it is with holy oil that the little lambs approaching baptism must be purified. With this oil have been consecrated priests, prophets and kings who became illustrious and wore the crown; with this oil are anointed the simple lambs that become the sons of the Father in heaven. It was prefigured for us by Moses in the desert, and its mystery, now fulfilled, has been transmitted to us by King David; and here, in the Church, the little lambs are signed that have come to baptism." [59]

Therefore, the celebration of baptism, studied in the liturgy of the catechumens, sums up God's plan and the economy of the covenant. That is the main source of its symbolism. It is easy to see its richness, its dynamism and its pastoral possibilities, but there is more. From the theological point of view, the relationship that distinguishes and unites the liturgy of the covenant and the rite of the water leads us to reflect upon the structure of this sacrament. Closer to the structure of the sacraments of penance and marriage than would seem at first sight, it appears as the completion of a gesture made by man—though anticipated by God—through a saving act of Christ; it appears as the fulfillment of the first covenant in the baptismal memorial of the passion and resurrection.

[58] Ps. 44 (45), 8-9.
[59] J. Assemani, *loc. cit.*, II, pp. 234-35; H. Denzinger, *loc. cit.*, I, p. 286.

Alois Stenzel, S.J./*Frankfurt, West Germany*

Temporal and Supra-Temporal in the History of the Catechumenate and Baptism

Preliminary Observation

My concern is with the main outline of the history of the catechumenate and adult baptism and not so much with the rite as actually administered. The more important individual rites and structural elements are examined elsewhere in this volume. However, I should explain how this theme will be approached. The juxtaposition of "temporal and supra-temporal" is certainly not meant to suggest a disinterested contrasting of one with the other; it is, rather, a question of showing the relevance for today of the body of living experience.

Confidence that the liturgy of baptism as we now have it[1] is on the whole still appropriate will affect what I have to say. The word "temporal" in the title is used to indicate that the article will include the critical comments made possible today by historical distance and required by pastoral commitment. Some aspects of the catechumenate and baptism, which might fall within the scope of the title, are not considered because of lack of space.

Vital Adaptation

The baptismal practice of the early centuries is proof of how

[1] R. Béraudy, "L'initiation chrétienne," in A. Martimort, *L'église en prière* (Paris, 1961), pp. 514-68; Th. Maertens, *Histoire et pastorale du catéchuménat et du baptême* (Saint André-de-Bruges, 1962); A. Stenzel, *Die Taufe. Eine genetische Erklaerung der Taufliturgie* (Baptism. A genetic explanation of the liturgy of baptism) (Innsbruck, 1958).

much the Church was aware of the obligation to concern herself with man's salvation in each new situation—with its uniquely
favorable points of contact, with its actual difficulties and needs.
The word "development"—in the sense of mere enlargement,
enrichment, becoming more complex—does not adequately express this diversity of practice.

Of course, there was development of this type. The rite was
considerably developed from an almost casual procedure suggested in Acts 10, 47 ("Can anyone forbid water for baptizing
these people who have received the Holy Spirit just as we have?")
to the more heterogeneously developed ritual at the end of the
2nd century (which Tertullian,[2] nevertheless, described as "simple but magnificent"), up to the rich, elaborate ceremonial of
today. Now, apart from the fact that this growth did not always
proceed in accordance with the avowed direction of its own
origins, there is nothing in such a very natural process to cause
surprise. What is astounding is the extent to which the Church
was always ready to adapt herself by shifting the emphasis, by
fresh combinations of traditional elements, by an unequivocal
renunciation of what had become superfluous and unusable.

This can be demonstrated. A question of supreme pastoral
importance (the answer to which is bound to affect the procedure) is: "Who fulfills the conditions for admission to baptism?" Accounts of baptism such as those of Acts 21, 41 and 8,
26-40 demand nothing more than faith, in response to the
kerygma. And this is not because there had not yet been time
to "invent" the catechumenate; examples of it were available.
It has always been assumed that the *Two Ways* schema of the
Didache goes back to the Jewish practice of instruction, and
recent studies have given us very precise information about the
lengthy postulancy and novitiate (to use terminology with which
we are familiar) of the Essenes, the people of Qumran. The
simple fact is that the Church was aware of her power to admit
anyone into the community of believers as soon as he had com-

[2] *De bapt. 2 (Corp. Christ.* 1, 277).

pleted his conversion to Christ Jesus who "fulfills" salvation history. In principle, and under the same conditions, the same procedure could be followed today.

As the Church grew, instruction—distinct from the kerygma —became necessary before baptism. The Church more and more examined the riches of her faith and rightly demanded that total attachment to Christ should be proved by longer initiation and tested by the acceptance of definite articles of faith. In addition, the Church, equipping herself for an unforeseeable history and moving more and more away from the native soil of Judaism in her institutions and in her community life, had to assure herself that the candidate for baptism also accepted this aspect of his conversion with all the social dimensions in sharply defined character. This was something that absolutely required time. The practice that then arose soon became the rule: after acceptance of the kerygma came instruction over a longer period. Here, particularly, the "teachers", mentioned frequently and as a matter of course, have their (*Sitz im Leben*) place in the life of the community (Acts 13, 1; 1 Cor. 12, 28f.; Heb. 6, 1).

From here it was only a short step to the ecclesial-official, institutional catechumenate[3] (certainly established by about 200). It was the reaction required of the Church when faced with the danger to doctrine that arose not least from the schools over which she had no control.[4] From then on teachers in the catechumenate required the approbation of the Church. The fact that candidates were usually kept for several (generally three) years in the catechumenate was again the result of alert adaptation to a changed situation. The people who were being led toward baptism were pagans who lacked the experience of "education in Christ", who lived in a polity that either placed a Christian

[3] B. Capelle, "L'introduction du catéchuménat à Rome," in *Rech. théol. anc. méd.* 5 (1933), pp. 129-54; A. Turck, "Aux origines du catéchuménat," in *Rev. sc. phil. et théol.* 48 (1964), pp. 20-31.

[4] G. Bardy, "Les écoles romaines au second siècle," in *Rev. Hist. Eccl.* 28 (1932), pp. 501-32.

life in extraordinary temptation or even (in the time of the State-Church) made it difficult to obtain an assurance about their motives—almost inevitably mixed.

This last situation, which determined the character of the subsequent age, deserves further consideration. It led first of all to a flowering of the "classical catechumenate" (largely determined by the canons of Hippolytus). There was no lack of candidates for baptism. In fact they kept a richly structured, thoroughly regulated institution running full time. But very soon there was a lack of people who really wanted baptism as opposed to the merely civil advantage and minimal relationship to the State-Church. The Church rose to the occasion. She did not succumb to the weight of an established institution, but abandoned this catechumenate that had degenerated to a religiously irrelevant queue of the many who knew on which side their bread was buttered. What the Church regarded as indispensable by way of testing, she now shifted into the final phase of the catechumenate.

Originally, a person was admitted to the catechumenate as *electus*—that is, as one whose successful probation had been confirmed and who was therefore "elected" and who now had only (as we might say today) to make his "baptismal retreat". This second phase, coinciding with Lent (and certainly exercising an influence on the gradual extension of the Lenten period), took over all the indispensable functions of the old-style catechumenate.

Augustine was certainly right in saying that the time for personal formation was too short,[5] but the Church could rely on the formative power of post-baptismal life in the community. Those baptized in infancy—a practice that became more frequent—were wholly dependent on this.

Further evidence could be adduced to show that the Church deliberately adapted her baptismal procedure and kept complete control. Thus, for example, she abandoned a showpiece like the

---

[5] Augustine takes a stand for moral probation as a requirement for admission to baptism in his *De fide et operibus*.

scrutiny rite once it became a useless procedure. Faced with the necessity of dealing with pagans (as in the mission to the Germanic tribes) she resolutely pushed the ceremonial elements into second place and gave kerygma and instruction their former predominance. All this should be an example to us. If we are justified in speaking of a "post-Christian age", then a return to a genuine catechumenate for adults is absolutely necessary.

That there is need for constant alertness is shown by the unfortunate absence of a baptismal ritual especially constructed to suit the needs of infant baptism. The very poverty-stricken adaptation—with its preference for, and accumulation of, those elements that remain most suited to the child's inevitable passivity—can hardly be regarded as such. The consequences are serious.

We have failed to compensate for this passivity in the rite. Perhaps this might have given suitable expression (an allusion would suffice) to the "faith of the Church", and could have actively engaged parents, sponsors and the parish as a whole. This crippled form of administering baptism must bear its full measure of blame for the notion that liturgy = official ecclesiastical ceremonies. Since rites have been retained (e.g., abjurations and profession of faith) which are simply not adapted to the situation of an infant, such a continual violation of the "truthfulness of the sign" (which is so important in the light of the *Constitution on the Sacred Liturgy*) cannot go on at all without weakening the force of the sacrament as sign. Meanwhile the category of sacrament-cause remains foremost in our minds. When we recall the fact that in treatises of sacramental theology baptism has always been regarded as the "model" sacrament, it is impossible to estimate the consequences too seriously.

Sacrament of Faith

We know how baptism in a special way has acquired the title of "sacrament of faith", not only since Augustine,[6] but even —in fact, if not in name—[7] in Tertullian. It will be worthwhile

---

[6] *Ep.* 98, 9 (*Corp. Script. Eccl. Lat.* 34, 531).

[7] *De paen.* VI, 16 (*Corp. Christ.* 1, 331).

to consider the meaning of both "sacrament" and "faith" in this context.

Whether we talk of faith or *metanoia,* unless the reality it designates is present, the basic requirement of a candidate for baptism is not fulfilled. But if the condition is fulfilled for that person, "what is to prevent his being baptized?" (cf. Acts 8, 36). Baptisms administered without delay prove the same point. Everything else is secondary.

Is faith existentially and properly summed up in the words: "Lord, I believe; help my unbelief" (Mk. 9, 24)? Does the theologian require at most an implicit belief? Does the Church leave it at that or does she require a more explicit assent and therefore arrange for instruction before baptism? All this belongs to the "economy" of the administration of baptism, which of course can be handled differently in different situations. What is decisive is that the person who has accepted the kerygma and become a "disciple" (Mt. 28, 19) must "believe that Jesus Christ is the Son of God" (Acts 8, 37). This is the minimum requirement for admission to baptism.

This is the attitude that inspired Tertullian's view[8] (we should not be deceived by his rather moralizing tone): "We are not plunged into the water in order to stop sinning, but because we have stopped sinning, since we are already washed at heart." Augustine takes the same stand in *De fide et operibus.* He is not concerned, for example, with a theologically indefensible, exaggerated estimate of the moral worthiness of the candidate. (Augustine is certainly the last person to be suspected of friendliness toward Catharism.) He insists on a living faith that must be proven by works. The same idea lies behind the introductory dialogue of the present-day baptismal ritual. When the question "What do you seek?" is answered with "The Faith", this has never been understood as a sought-after and not-yet-available faith. Faith here means the *sacramentum fidei*—that is, baptism. Believing is the fundamental condition.

The service which the Church still has to provide for the

---

[8] *De paen.* VI, 17 (*Corp. Christ.* 1, 331).

ripening of this faith and which she considers it proper to provide even before baptism, according to the candidate's situation, must not be allowed to obscure the importance of this observation. It holds good in any situation. Even today, although we have not had a catechumenate for centuries, we might indeed find a pre-catechumenate necessary. The objection to this as "exaggeration and rigorism" is easy to formulate but false.

Let us now consider the "sacrament". If it is true that there are not two ways to the God of grace (one by way of faith, the other by way of the sacraments), but only the one; if it is true that the sacrament is the inwardness of faith given corporeal expression in the visibility of the Church; if it is true that such a sacramental event is not merely an appended "visible word", but the Church's most profound self-realization—then the whole way of faith in the Church must be followed sacramentally. In other words, baptism as the sacrament of faith must be an event coextensive with the stages of the development of faith. And that is just what history shows it to be.

There is certainly no clearer proof of this than the fact that catechumens were counted as really "in the Church". It was expressed both in the familiar metaphor of the Fathers that the catechumen "is already in the womb of the Church, but not yet born" and in the use of the name "Christian" to include catechumens and (full) believers,[9] which then logically led to the fact that in many orders of baptism the first step toward making a catechumen (*ad catechumen faciendum*) was expressed less formally and therefore more fully as *ad Christianum faciendum* (to make a Christian).

This is not merely a question of a very vague notion of membership (pardonably so at the time and difficult even today to define, as the discussions at Vatican Council II have shown). What is involved rather is a conception of the greatest significance and fruitfulness. It implies both the decisive importance of

[9] Augustine, *Sermo* 46, 31 (*Corp. Christ.* 41, 557): "Are you pagan or Christian?" He replies: "I'm a Christian." He is, because he is a sheep of God. You may ask him whether he is not still a catechumen.

salvific faith[10] and the possibility and necessity of its sacramental character as realized in the Church. The catechumenate
is not an arbitrarily concocted, preparatory study course into
which—reasonably enough, in view of man's body-soul unity—
a few rites have been incorporated. The catechumenate is not
best understood merely as education and certainly not simply to
be defined as preparation for baptism.

The ecclesial-sacramental quality of the catechumenate is so
rich that its importance is not adequately expressed by saying
that the progressive ripening of faith occurs "in virtue" of the
sacrament of baptism (the sacrament itself being considered as
distinct from this process). We must say, rather, that the sacrament of faith itself is "extended" insofar as the Church considers necessary an interval between "coming to believe" and
the final sealing (Tertullian's expression) of that belief in the
baptismal bath. A theory of this kind is not invalidated by the
fact that the Church in principle (and certainly only in rare
cases) can dispense with this "extension".

There is no reason why we should not now return to this
conception of the sacrament of faith. Vatican Council II discussed the question of Church membership deliberately from
the standpoint of its full realization. Unlike the encyclical *Mystici
corporis,* it avoided setting up exclusive frontiers between members and non-members. Since the existence of grace outside the
visible Church is not in dispute, the intention can only have been
to make ecclesiality (and therefore also sacramentality) a less
rigid, more open concept, thus liberating it from the narrower
definition implied in the encyclical.

This, too, is of pastoral importance. If the catechumen has
ecclesial status, we need not be so concerned about the effects
of baptism and can pay more attention to the laws of the liturgical action. There is a breathing space, sufficient to leave time

---

[10] We might note here in what an unobtrusive and balanced way, but
also how imperturbably, the Constitutions of Vatican II on the Church
and the liturgy put in second place everything which—as distinct from
the Church as salvation-community—must come under the heading of
"institution".

for the individual's ripening. We can unhurriedly establish the rhythm of the individual ritual observances (exorcism, abjuration, profession of faith, etc.), so that a really spontaneous, mature inwardness enters into each of these "protestations of faith" (a key concept of Aquinas' sacramental theology). Baptism itself can then easily be delayed, for example, until Easter. Certainly more could be said concerning this, but these suggestions may suffice here.

The positive significance of the sacred signs with which the Church has paved the way to baptism has not always been properly appreciated. We also can learn from this neglect. In the course of history they have consistently been reduced to ceremonial fill-in material without theological significance; their essential quality as signs were given second place, to be understood too one-sidedly as mere instruments rather than signs. Two major remedies might be applied to this situation.

First, a return to an essential economy (one symbol is better than several) and simultaneously to the integrity of the outward form (immersion instead of a paltry sprinkling) would help. We must trust the inexhaustible representational power of the great symbols. (We could learn from the cigarette advertisement that publicizes the purity and freshness of its products with the aid of the picture of a bubbling mountain brook.)

Secondly, we should be more aware of the role of the Word, as opposed to the mere ritual element in a sacrament.[11] It will have to be discussed elsewhere what effect this has in practice on the biblical setting of the interpretative words, the choice of pericopes and the insertion of services of the Word.

Baptism—Permanent Dimension of the Christian Life

This heading should dispel any suggestion that baptism could be regarded as the primary and indispensable condition of Christian life which, once fulfilled, can be progressively ignored as we grow older and wiser in the faith. This error is not merely

[11] Augustine, *In. Ev. Jo.,* tract. 80, 3 (*Corp. Christ.* 36, 529): "If words are added to the rite, we have a sacrament".

hypothetical. History shows that the danger was appreciated and that every attempt was made to ward it off. The urgent warning in Hebrews 6, 4 could be cited: "It is impossible to restore again to repentance those who have once been enlightened." It was understood that "being in constant *metanoia*" was a post-baptismal description of the Christian as such.

Baptism was therefore called *sphragis, sigillum,* a sealing, a dedication to *metanoia*.[12] The formula was created as a command, valid for life: "Preserve the seal of baptism".[13] All life was subsequently seen as a consequence of this first commitment. The observances of "normal" Christian life and penitential exercises were all linked with the abandonment of the devil and sin which took place at baptism;[14] the more extraordinary acts of the Christian life—martyrdom,[15] the entry into religion[16]—were also linked directly or indirectly with baptism.

Reflections like these show how much remains to be desired in the ritual as we now have it. We must also regret the fact that the "scrutinies" are carried out almost exclusively as a retrospective examination of the candidate. Their force as a sign is weakened because they fail to show that baptism implies a permanent way of life and constant commitment. The exorcisms, too—the purifying and sanctifying intervention of the merciful God, to be received as a gift from above—ought to be presented in such a way as to transport the reality of the covenant (which is, first of all, God's initiative) into the individual history of salvation. In them the kingdom of God appears as having come (Jn. 12, 31: "Now is the judgment of this world; now shall the ruler of this world be cast out"), and it does so in such a way that the person

[12] Origen, *In Lc. hom.* 21 (*Greich. christl. Schriftst.* 9, 139, 20ff); Tertullian, *De paen.* VI, 17 (Corp. Christ. 1, 331).

[13] *2 Clem.* 6, 9; 7, 6; 8, 6 (Funk, *Patres Apostolici* I [Tübingen, 1901], 192, 194); Origen, *In Jerem. hom.* 2, 3 (*GCS* 3, 19, 22).

[14] Origen, *In Jo. comm.* 6, 33 (*GCS* 4, 143, 1); *idem, In Exod. hom.* 2, 2 (*GCS* 6, 254, 24ff).

[15] *Idem, In Jo. comm.* 6, 56 (*GCS* 4, 165, 18ff); *In Mt. comm. frgm.* 403 (*GCS* 12, 170); *Protr.* 17 (*P.G.* 11, 585A).

[16] *Dict. Arch. chrét. et Lit.* I, 2604-15: "Apotactites".

submitting to the exorcisms has to accept the duty of a lifelong trial of "mind and heart" (cf. Ps. 7, 10), letting himself be initiated completely into "prayer and fasting" without which temptations cannot be overcome. In general, he knows that he is bound permanently to maintain the light against the darkness within him and around him.

A further point that should be mentioned is that the baptismal ritual fails to express adequately what might be called the "baptismal paraclesis". It is true that the eschatological note is there. But for the rest of his life, while he is living out his "time of the Church", the individual lacks the encouragement needed in so many situations to have recourse to the strength that baptism offers. It is often said that the message contained in the blessing of baptismal water should be heard if possible at every individual baptism. Here, in fact, would be a good place for the paraclesis. It should be a holy and sobering initiation into the constancy of a "life hidden with Christ in God" (Col. 3, 3) and into the unavoidable experience that we have died to sin—although sin itself is far from dead. From it we would gain the comfort that it is not by the effort of human goodwill that the imperatives of the Christian life are to be realized in the midst of constant temptation, but rather by turning to God's unrepentant bestowal of baptismal grace.

The practice of the early Church might also be mentioned, for it made the community experience baptism as a permanent dimension. There was, for example, the formative power of a Lent in which baptismal themes were predominant.[17] These ought again to be revived. Nor should it be simply a question of the individual choosing to look back to his baptism: he should become more profoundly aware of it through the community's understanding of baptism. The history of liturgy knows such an institution by the term *pascha annotinum*. To revive this would certainly be of the greatest value for baptismal faith.

[17] A. Chavasse, "Signification baptismale du Carême et de l'octave pascale" in *La Maison-Dieu* 58 (1959), pp. 27-38.

Baptism—Sacrament of the Church

This, of course, has been my theme all along, but some aspects need particular emphasis.

Practical appreciation of baptism's considerable ecclesial quality certainly needs renewal. Indeed, it would have been singular if infant baptism, which has dominated baptismal practice for more than a thousand years, had not caused an impoverishment of this quality.

What we mean is this. In the long period between receiving baptism in infancy and the development from that moment to conscious Christian living, all the work of education—including instruction for confirmation, first communion, etc.—must be accomplished. It is small wonder that baptism was certainly recognized as the indispensable, basic sacrament, with sublime effects that wholly and entirely justify its administration as soon as possible (*quam primum*); on the other hand, baptism was seen in practice as a presupposition of an ecclesial life that was to come later, merely a necessary first grade, necessary before ascending to the second, third, etc.

In regard to adults, the traditional view must again be asserted: namely, that baptism (together with its *per-fectio,* which is confirmation) plus the eucharist make up the one initiation. If this normal continuity of administration is observed, it brings out the fact that to be capable of baptism is to be capable of the central sacrament of the eucharist and thus of an ecclesial existence complete in every respect. Obviously, then, the requirements are high and, as already indicated, there arises the question of the catechumenate (and eventually even pre-catechumenate). This is not archeologism: baptism is not to be had more cheaply.

Of timeless validity is the desire shown in the baptismal practice of the early Church that the Church should be understood as the "sacrament" of the restoration of the world by grace. Concretely, this is the effort to turn into living and enduring experience the fact that the frontier between those who are far off and those who are near, between those outside and those within the Church, has been crossed. The machinery, certainly time-conditioned in its forms, is well known: greater demands on admission to the catechumenate and discipline of the secret, progressive initiation through the "transmissions" in stages of the Creed, Our Father and Gospel.

And today? Expressions such as "dialogue with the world", "anonymous Christianity", etc., are regarded with suspicion in some quarters, and they certainly have their dangers. The old machinery cannot be revived in its entirety. But some kind of rite of "transition" seems to be required. The passage from the world outside Christianity to the full life of the Christian community must find liturgical expression. Negatively, we might say that a certain reserve is indispensable, at least in regard to the celebration of the eucharist. Positively, even today we might find it hard to discover a better way of bringing out progress toward baptism than the "transmissions" of bible, profession of faith and the Our Father.

The permanent importance of the office of baptismal sponsor should be obvious. Its functions in the early practice of the Church[18] (sponsor at first reception, mentor during the catechumenate, and again witness of admission to baptism) are absolutely required from the nature of the case. In any event, today we ought to be very alert to the fact that this is always directly a question of faith, not of morality. To be on the way to the Church is not to be seeking acceptance into a society of people of morally higher status.

The ecclesial significance of the sponsor deserves to be emphasized. Today more than ever it is essential[19] that "the Church" (not her professionals, her officials) should be a missionary Church, for she is present to the "world" only through the "Christian on the spot". Above all, the living Church can

[18] M. Dujarier, *Le parrainage des adultes aux trois premiers siècles de l'Eglise* (Paris, 1962); M. van Molle, "Les fonctions du parrainage en Occident," in *Par. Lit.* 46 (1964), pp. 121-46.

[19] As for the beginnings, cf. A. von Harnack, *Die Mission und Ausbreitung des Christentums in den ersten drei Jahrhunderten* I (Leipzig, ⁴1924), pp. 332-79.

be experienced by the catechumen only by live contact with real people. (How would it be possible, for instance, to learn about *aggiornamento* from books?) It is not simply a question of the force of example. "Infectious" contact with the sponsor (and, obviously, with his family and his circle of friends) is an indispensable means of coming to know the Church.

Finally, I should mention one further aspect of baptism that in the passage of time has been lost and now needs reasserting—the community character of the way to baptism and of baptism itself. The liturgy of this sacrament of the Church must be something not only of interest to the community and open to it, but should also be something that actually requires its presence.

Michel Dujarier/*Cotonou, Dahomey*

Sponsorship

" **C**atechumens who, moved by the Holy Spirit, seek with explicit intention to be incorporated into the Church are by that very intention joined to her," states Vatican Council II. "With love and solicitude Mother Church already embraces them as her own." [1] This maternal solicitude has led to a rediscovery of adult sponsorship in the current renewal of the catechumenate. Christian initiation should, in fact, "be taken care of not only by catechists and priests, but by the entire community of the faithful, especially by the sponsors. Thus, from the very outset, the catechumens will feel that they belong to the People of God".[2]

This rediscovery of the role of sponsorship in the Church is far from complete. It would be more accurate to say that research into it is being carried out. Just as it is difficult to fit life into formulas, so one hesitates to set out the steps taken along a still incomplete course. But certain recent works do indicate how different communities envisage the function of sponsor.[3]

---

[1] *Dogmatic Constitution on the Church*, n. 14 (Glen Rock, N.J.: Paulist Press, 1965).

[2] *Decree on the Church's Missionary Activity*, n. 14, and *Decree on the Ministry and Life of Priests*, n. 6 (Glen Rock, N.J.: Paulist Press, 1966).

[3] Cf., for example, J. Dournes, "Le parrain, témoin de l'Eglise," in *Vie Spir.* 515 (1965), pp. 399-408; *Anon,* "Le parrainage," in *Docu-*

They clearly describe the Church's care to welcome those whom the Spirit is awakening to faith, to understand those who are seeking for God and to help them on their way to him.

The study of the historical evolution of sponsorship has barely started. Its origins have been examined,[4] but the investigation still needs to be pursued: first, in time, by carrying the study from the 5th century to the present day, and then in space, by observing the customs of the Eastern Churches and the practice of the missions and new Churches.

Meanwhile, on the pastoral level, renewal is being sought through a greater *authenticity,* reacting against usages that have become stale through familiarity and thus lost the deep value of their human content.

While in no way sharing the view of some 19th-century writers that catechumens have no need of sponsors because they are adults, one must admit that sponsorship has very often been reduced to the status of a "liturgical lie".[5] Can a man called at the last minute to accompany a neophyte, of whose progress toward faith he is completely ignorant, really be considered a genuine sponsor? And what about the mission catechist who often acts as godfather to dozens of young converts over whose future development he can have absolutely no control?

There is, therefore, a need for efforts to restore an effective form of sponsorship. To be effective, it must be exercised during the whole of the catechumen's preparation for baptism, supporting him in his progress toward a living faith. It must also be lived in a personal relationship between two people on sufficiently close terms to be able to engage in genuine discussion.

Yet, even when this personal relationship exists, the fact remains that one person is not enough to establish all the conditions favorable to a true conversion. The whole Church must

---

ments de Service National du Catéchuménat 26 (Paris, 1964); Audollent, "L'entourage des convertis," *ibid.* 32 (1965).

[4] M. Dujarier, *Le parrainage des adultes aux trois premiers siècles de l'Eglise* (Paris, 1962); B. de Guchteneere, *Le parrainage des adultes aux 4° et 5° siècles de l'Eglise* (Rome: Greg. Univ., 1962).

[5] A. Stenzel, *Die Taufe* (Innsbruck, 1958) p. 287.

help the newcomer to the People of God.[6] Without denying that the role of the actual sponsor is indispensable, it is important to recognize that the whole Christian community has a true sponsoring responsibility—what might be called "collective sponsorship"—provided this is understood to mean not one sponsor in charge of many converts, but rather the feeling of sponsorship that all the faithful should have who, in one way or another, make up the human entourage of the catechumen. The expression "communal sponsorship" would seem to be better than the rather ambiguous term "collective sponsorship".

This double effort—which present-day pastoral activity is, as it were, spontaneously finding necessary—reflects the conclusions of historical research to an amazing degree.

Sponsorship, contrary to what one might think, did not originate in the customs surrounding infant baptism, but rather in those of the preparation of adults for baptism. (C. Brusselmans has shown how the sponsorship of infants, which was originally a resource only used in the case of orphans, eventually came to usurp a function that clearly belongs by right to the parents.[7]) Sponsors were originally those convinced Christians of the early centuries who persuaded their friends or colleagues to be converted, and who, after they had brought them to the catechumenate, continued to lend them brotherly assistance until they were fully initiated. Far from being the latest arrivals on the scene, they were the first movers in the process of conversion and their function remained of primordial importance, even during the catechesis.[8]

Besides giving a clearer idea of the role of the personal sponsor, historical investigation also helps in discovering the ecclesial dimension of sponsorship. The whole Church, the Mother of the faithful, has to bring men the Good News and then welcome,

[6] Cf. J. Cellier, "Catéchumenes et communauté chrétienne," in *Maison-Dieu* 71 (1962), pp. 142-50.

[7] C. Brusselmans, *Les fonctions de parrainage des enfants aux premiers siècles de l'Eglise* (Institut supérieur de pastorale catéchétique de Paris, 1962).

[8] M. Dujarier, *op. cit.,* p. 377.

sustain and educate those who become members of the People of the covenant. Even at those times when the catechumenate tended to disappear, bishops such as Cesarius of Arles were still there to remind people that it was not the sponsors alone who were responsible, but all Christians, whose duty it was to encourage the candidates for baptism by their words and example.[9] And the custom of not accepting anyone for baptism without the consent of the local Christian community remained in force for a long time.[10]

The sponsor must be at the same time a witness-guarantor and a father-guide.[11] He takes on this dual task in the name of the Church vis-à-vis the catechumen, and at the same time in the name of the catechumen vis-à-vis the Church.

As a witness to Christ, he witnesses in his daily life primarily for those men of goodwill who are seeking God, and he will continue to do this throughout their catechumenate, since converts need to see the Gospel actually being lived by men like themselves to be sure that the Church really is the bearer of the riches she claims to possess and distribute. But he is also a witness giving evidence to the Christian community of the serious intention of the candidate for conversion at each stage of his journey, especially his entry into the catechumenate and his reception of baptism.

As a guide, the sponsor is responsible for introducing his godchild into the City of God, showing him the usages and customs of the People of which he is becoming a member. This is a true "spiritual fatherhood", exercised in the name of the Church. Reciprocally, he could also be said to be the guide responsible for showing the Church to the unevangelized world to which the catechumen is humanly bound.

These functions, of course, do not belong exclusively to the sponsor, or even primarily to him; they have their roots in the mission of the whole Christian community. All Christians have

[9] Sermon 200, 6 (Corp. Christ. 104, 811).
[10] J. Moschus, *Le pré spirituel*, p. 207 (*P.G.* 87, 3097-3100).
[11] M. Dujarier, *op. cit.*, pp. 49-62.

to take part in the "maternal care" of the Church, and all should feel concerned in the actions that will introduce and mature new subjects in the People of the covenant. But this does not mean that the canonical sponsor is unnecessary. Far from it! By himself he is nothing; he acts as the representative of the family of God of which he is a living member, and the responsibility he takes on himself is only an expression of the sponsoring responsibility of the whole community. But his part is still indispensable, because the Church makes him not merely her delegate, but the visible and efficacious sign of her sponsoring action.

Thus there are good reasons for the present-day pastoral concern to establish a genuine sponsorship in its two dimensions: individual and communal. The aim is to discover the true human entourage of a sympathizer as soon as he makes his first approaches, to put other Christians in touch with him, however imperfect they may be, and to give them a gradually increasing sense of their responsibility as sponsors toward him. This means educating Christians toward this sense of responsibility, particularly in places where Christians themselves have never experienced a sense of genuine community help. To avoid artificiality, the convert should then choose, from among these Christians in his entourage, the person who is to be his "spiritual father" during his catechumenate and even after his baptism.

Efforts are being made to discover the proper relationship between the catechumenate and Catholic Action,[12] and, on a still wider front, between the catechumenate and the whole missionary effort of the Church. At the same time that the catechumen is introduced to corporate apostolic action in the Church, the Church's missionary activity as a whole should be introduced to the individual who is progressing toward the Church.

These notes on the subject of sponsorship—for they can be called no more than notes—show that the whole question is still

[12] Cf. M. Saudreau, "La J.O.C. mouvement catéchuménal," in *Masses Ouvrières* 179 (1961), pp. 39-76; G. Renaudin, "Le parrainage," in *Catéchuménat de Paris* (1965).

at a very early and tentative stage of development. Perhaps it must always be so. It is surely more normal to be engaged in continual research than to take up some fixed position that will soon become outdated. But research does show up certain main lines along which it would appear that our thinking must develop. There is a real need for an effective system of personal sponsorship to guide the catechumen on his first steps toward conversion, and for an ecclesial sponsorship which, without supplanting the irreplaceable role of the personal sponsor, will restore its full value by making it the special expression of a real community welcome.

The first tentative efforts being made in this direction in the personal field already give some indication of the immense benefits that a revaluation of sponsorship will bring to the catechumenate. But this is far from the only benefit, for the whole Church will benefit from being invited to a more genuine response to the missionary requirements of her maternal care for a world that is today in full development and in which the Holy Spirit is constantly making his appeal.

Thierry Maertens, O.S.B. / *Bruges, Belgium*

History and Function of the Three Great Pericopes: *The Samaritan Woman, The Man Born Blind, The Raising of Lazarus*

Thanks to the researches of Antoine Chavasse, we are now able to understand the formularies of Lent.[1] Working steadily back through the centuries to a date before 384, the Strasbourg professor has discovered that in this period the preparation for Easter was dominated by three important readings. They were attached to the three Sundays which at that time constituted the sole preparation: John 4 (the woman of Samaria), John 9 (the man born blind) and John 11 (the raising of Lazarus). Perhaps a fourth reading should be added: John 8 (Abraham), to which Chavasse does not appear to attach the importance it seems to have had in the liturgies of Milan and Benevento and in the Gallican liturgy.

Although it is only an hypothesis, one might suppose that

---

[1] The author's chief articles are: "La structure du Carême et les lectures des messes quadragésimales dans la liturgie romaine," in *Maison-Dieu* 31 (1952), pp. 76-119; "Le Carême romain et les scrutins prébaptismaux avant le IXe siècle," in *Rech. Sc. relig.* (1948), pp. 325-81. The author has given a summary of his studies in *L'Eglise en prières, Introduction à la liturgie* (Paris: Ed. Desclée et Cie, 1965), pp. 720-32. Appreciation of his work as a whole is found in J. Jungmann, "Die Quadragesima in den Forschungen von Antoine Chavasse," in *Arch. f. Liturg.* (1957), pp. 84-95. A popular presentation of his ideas can be found in Th. Maertens, "Le liturgie du Carême est-elle encore pour notre temps?" (Bruges: Ed. Biblica, 1958), and in A. Aubry, "Points de repère pour une explication génétique du Carême romain," in *Assemblée du Seigneur* 21 (1963), pp. 7-22.

these three or four readings go back to an ancient system of consecutive readings of St. John in preparation for Easter. But in any case it is certain that at the time when written evidence first appears, these readings had been to some extent taken over by the 4th-century catechumenal preparation and used more directly in preparation for baptism. Transferred from the Sundays to which they originally belonged to the ferias where they now appear (third Friday, fourth Wednesday and fourth Friday), they have shared the development of the celebration of the scrutinies: at first solemn (in the 4th century), then gradually pushed back into the week, when infant baptism took the place of the baptism of adults (6th century?). However far back we go in the liturgical formula, we find these readings, each coupled with a reading from the Old Testament, designed to place the Gospel story in the framework of salvation history. The story of the rock of living water (Num. 20) forms a pendant to the story of Jacob's well (Jn. 4). The theme of purification (Is. 1) introduces the story of the man born blind, washing away his uncleanness at Siloe (Jn. 9), while the raising of the widow's son (1 Kg. 17) prepares for that of Lazarus (Jn. 11). The theme of "light" and "darkness" in Isaiah 44, 8-15 could have helped in the understanding of John 8 (cf. v. 12), insofar as the latter figured in the ancient Lenten lectionary of Rome. In the same period, no doubt, and in any case before these readings were transferred to the ferias, they were used to form the texts of the communion antiphons, still in place today, which reveal to the baptized the essential dimensions of the eucharist: well-spring of eternal life (Jn. 4, 13-14: third Friday), expression of faith in the Lord (Jn. 9, 6. 7. 15. 35. 38: fourth Wednesday) and source of resurrection (Jn. 11, 33-34: fourth Friday).[2] Finally, the three chief readings inspired the composition of proper prefaces, edited only in the 9th century, but certainly of earlier date.[3]

[2] Note that the author of this antiphon has neatly inserted the text of John 20, 11 (Magdalene weeping at the tomb of Christ), thus leading the believer to see through the tomb of Lazarus to the tomb of Christ, source of all life.

[3] The Roman sobriety of their style and their ancient latinity argue for the antiquity of these prefaces. But to support the conjectures of

For the sake of those readers who want to rediscover the religious climate of the ancient services, the texts of these three prefaces follow.[4]

THE WOMAN OF SAMARIA

It is truly right and good to give glory to you . . . through Christ our Lord: he who, in order to suggest the mystery of his weakness, sat wearied by the well, and asked the woman of Samaria to give him water to drink: he who, having created in her the gift of faith, deigned to be so athirst for her faith that by asking her for water to drink he kindled in her the fire of divine love. We therefore implore your infinite mercy that we, despising the dark depths of vices and leaving behind the pitcher of evil desires, may ever be athirst for you, the spring of life and source of goodness, and may please you through the observance of our fasts.

THE MAN BORN BLIND

It is truly right and good to give glory to you . . . through Christ our Lord: he who, by the illumination of his faith, scattered the darkness of this world, and by the mystery of his incarnation gave sight to the race of man, born blind from the womb of his first mother, and who made those who were bound in the slavery of a deserved damnation to be children of adoption. Through him we pray you that at his most just judgment we may be found such as we have become in the joyful new birth of saving

---

Chavasse we should know more about the sources of Alcuin's supplement to the Gregorian sacramentary (*P.G.* 121, 891-92).

[4] Translation by P. Journel, "Préfaces et oraisons de Carême," in *Notes de Past. Lit.* 36 (1962), pp. 21-22.

baptism, so that initiated by the remedy of his incarnation, washed by the water of the sacramental bath and beautified by a generous abstinence, we may attain to eternal joys.

LAZARUS

It is truly right and good to give glory to you . . . through Christ our Lord: he who is the unending day, the unfading light, the eternal glory, who bade his disciples to walk in the light so as to escape the darkness and to arrive happily at the homeland of light; he who, in the weakness of his human nature, wept for Lazarus, who by the power of his godhead restored to life and raised up the human race, buried under the fourfold weight of sin. Through him we pray that the observance of the fast may deliver us from the bonds of sin, bring us to the happiness of eternal life and cause us to be numbered in the company of the saints.

The theology of these prefaces is clear. Christ here appears both in the weakness of his human nature and in the power of his godhead. The one makes him share in man's poverty, the other enables him to grant to every man that faith represented by the living water, the life or the light. But Christ's incarnation is continued in the Church and in her sacramental economy; baptism, the eucharist and the Lenten fast come to the aid of our frailty and sin, to illuminate them in the faith and to promise them glory. As regards baptism, no mention is made of the catechumens, undoubtedly because they were no longer in the church when the preface was sung. In fact, at the moment when they were dismissed, or a little before it, the celebrant pronounced over them a formula of exorcism or "scrutiny".[5] We

[5] A. Chavasse was also concerned to discover the other elements of the formulary (*Rech. Sc. rel.*, 1948, pp. 365-66). The elements discovered as the result of these conjectures do not concern us, as they do not mention the Gospel texts. But that is not the case with the scrutiny forms, which I am about to analyze.

have only to read the rite for the baptism of adults to find at least one formula that could have served as a scrutiny during the offices *De caeco nato* and *De Lazaro;* it is found in n. 38 of the *Ritual of the Catechumenate and Baptism of Adults* (1962 edition):

I adjure you, unclean spirit, by the Father and the Son and the Holy Spirit, to come out of these servants of God. For he who commands you is he who opened the eyes of the man born blind and raised Lazarus from the tomb when he had been dead four days.

The catechumen therefore owes his conversion to the power of him who gave sight to the blind and restored life to Lazarus. It is certain, then, that two of the great primitive pericopes of Lent have influenced the baptismal ritual itself. Can we say the same of the gospel *De Samaritana* or the gospel *De Abraham?* Of course, the formula *Deus Abraham* in an exorcism of the Ritual (1962, n. 30) is not enough to provide evidence of this. But there is perhaps a more serious indication in the relation which once existed between *De Abraham* (at least the extract which survives on the fourth Saturday and treats of the relations between Christ and his Father) and the "tradition" or "handing over" of the *Our Father*. It seems, indeed, that this link between John 8, 12-20 and the *Our Father* is not as ancient as the other scrutinies, but it is true nonetheless that *De Abraham* played a scarcely less decisive role than the other three gospels in the primitive Lent and in the catechumenate of the 4th and 5th centuries.

I am not the first to express the hope that, in harmony with the *Constitution on the Sacred Liturgy* of Vatican Council II (n. 109), the Masses *De Samaritana, De caeco nato* and *De Lazaro* (and why not also *De Abraham?*) may be restored to their primitive places, with their full formularies, on the chief Sundays of Lent, and may also be celebrated as votive Masses at the catechumenal scrutinies which now prepare the adults and the welcoming communities at the baptisms of new Christians. This would provide a sort of pre-baptismal retreat on the subject of themes so essential to the Christian way, such as faith, water, light, life and the Father. The very fact that the liturgy of the Word would be completed by the actions or the "traditions" for the catechumens, and by the eucharist for the faithful, would thus have great significance by showing the former that their conversion is effected through the life of the latter. Finally, by the very presence of the Word and of the rite, the celebrations would accord the first place in conversion and in the progress of faith to the action of God.

Roger Béraudy, S.S./*Lyons, France*

Scrutinies and Exorcisms

"**S**crutiny" is the name given to the Lenten Masses during which the exorcisms are administered to those catechumens who are to receive baptism on the following Easter, and who on this account used to form the class of the "chosen". At Rome in the 4th and 5th centuries there were three services of scrutiny, appointed respectively for the third, fourth and fifth Sundays of Lent. The formulas then in use are preserved in the Gelasian sacramentaries.[1]

The purpose of this study is to examine the Gelasian formulas of exorcism, which differ in places from those now in use, and to determine their meaning.

I

THE CONTENT OF THE FORMULAS OF EXORCISM

Each of the three exorcisms comprised an exorcism over the men and another over the women, making a total of six formulas, and these in turn were divided into two elements, an intercession and an adjuration.

The prayers of intercession always start from a past action of

---

[1] Ed. L. Mohlberg (*Rerum ecclesiasticarum documenta,* Series major, fontes IV), Rome, 1964, pp. 44-46.

God and, arguing from this, they beg for a similar protection for the catechumens. Thus, the first exorcism over the men recalls the anticipating measures God took with regard to Israel's deliverance from the bondage of Egypt. The formula evokes God's manifestation on Mount Horeb, which made Moses the liberator of his people. Then, recalling that Yahweh sent an angel to watch over the Hebrews on their march to the desert, it prays for a similar favor for the catechumens, who must be guided to baptism.[2]

This request is resumed in the conclusion of the exorcism over the women at the first scrutiny. Here the prayer is based on the reminder of the homage which the "chosen" render to God by living according to his commandments ("God of all those who live righteously") and by confessing the faith "conceived" in their hearts by the doctrinal teaching they have received ("God, whom every tongue shall confess and to whom every knee shall bow, on earth and under the earth": cf. Phil. 2, 5-11).[3]

In the Gelasian, the exorcism over the men in the second scrutiny contains only a formula of adjuration. The present formula of intercession is an early 9th-century addition which bears the mark of an age when infants were baptized very soon after birth. For the corresponding exorcism over the women the Gelasian provides a special formula of intercession, distinct from that of the first exorcism over the men. Three figures of baptismal theology are here invoked: the deliverance of Israel from the slavery of Egypt, the promulgation of the Decalogue and the deliverance of Susanna from the machinations of her enemies. In this prayer God appears as the liberator who is asked to give present deliverance to the catechumens.

In contrast with the above, the two exorcisms of the third scrutiny begin with an authoritative adjuration, but reference to biblical precedents is not lacking. The sense of the divine intervention in favor of the catechumens is brought out in turn by the deliverance of Peter from the "waters of death" on the

[2] *Rituale Romanum* (RR), Tit. II, c. 4, p. 11, 21a.
[3] *Ibid.*, 23a.

lake of Tiberias (exorcism over the men), the cure of the man born blind and the raising of Lazarus (exorcism over the women). In these formulas Christ appears as the deliverer from death.[4]

Except in the second exorcism over the men, the adjuration always consists of the form, "Therefore, accursed devil".[5] This formula begins with three commands. Satan must acknowledge the sentence passed on him by Jesus Christ (cf. Jn. 12, 31; 16, 11). He must express his submission to the judgment which has stripped him of his power, by doing homage to the three divine Persons and by withdrawing from the catechumen. The reason for this withdrawal is our Lord's decision to call the catechumen to baptism ("Jesus Christ has deigned to call him to his holy grace and blessing and to the fountain of baptism"). Finally, the sign of the cross, with which the catechumen is marked, shows that the kingdom of God henceforth extends to him, so that Satan may not violate its frontiers.

The same ideas are resumed in the formula, "Hear, accursed Satan", in the second exorcism over the men.[6] The minister charges Satan to go out of the catechumen in virtue of the judgment that has sealed his defeat ("vanquished with your hate"). This departure is based on various reasons: on the one hand, the "chosen" is already attached to the heavenly truths that have been taught him during his catechumenate ("he already thinks on heavenly things"); on the other hand, he is preparing to renounce Satan and to enter into eternal life ("he is about to renounce you and the world and to live for a blessed immortality"). By this retreat Satan gives honor to the Holy Spirit, who carries out his sanctifying task in perfecting the Church ("that [the Spirit] may make perfect the holy temple and dwelling-place of God")[7] through baptism ("purifying his heart through the baptismal font").

[4] *Ibid.*, 35a, 38a.
[5] *Ibid.*, 21b.
[6] *Ibid.*, 28b.
[7] The expression, "the holy temple and the dwelling-place of God", has sometimes been understood of the catechumen, while the coming of the Spirit into that temple has been interpreted as confirmation.

II

THE MEANING OF THE EXORCISMS

By appealing to the action by which God leads his "chosen" to baptism, the formulas of intercession represent the exorcisms as interventions of God to prepare the catechumen for the sacrament of regeneration. The essential aim of this intervention is to "conjure" or expel Satan, the chief obstacle in the catechumen's path to baptism. In effect, because they link the "expulsion" of the devil with Christ's call to baptism, the forms of adjuration show that this call, by denouncing and condemning the wrong use that the sinner has made of his freedom, also unmasks and "conjures" in man the presence of a pre-human figure, who is hand-in-glove with his sin: Satan.

Man is not the absolute Evil, the Bad or the Wicked One; he is only the subordinate evildoer. The man who admits to being the author of evil discovers the reverse of this confession: namely, that evil is prior in time to the freedom that proposes it. Man's sin is never an absolute beginning, for evil always precedes itself. Whenever man in his turn begins it, in beginning it he finds and continues it. In all sin there is an element of passivity, of inclination and consent, for conscience is involved in it by its own covetousness. By preferring itself to others, every human conscience yields to a seduction of itself by itself, which makes a thing into the object of a desire.

This element of passivity, though it takes account of the tragic and radical note by which evil is marked, also enables us to understand that it does not belong to the essential condition of the created being. Finiteness, which is man's lot (since he exists only as multiple), is not the same as evil, any more than evil, for that matter, is finiteness. Between the two there is a hiatus, for evil is not identical with the plurality of human consciences; it lies in the fact that we are not what we ought to be, because we are self-satisfied, so that we isolate ourselves and oppose ourselves to others, instead of communicating with them. Finiteness is good in its origin; evil is contingent, although its presence is not explained by the sole action of man, since one aspect of evil cannot be curbed by human freedom.

The border-figure of the devil indicates the evil that is already there even when I commit it; it is the unposited reverse of a posited evil.[8] Satan is evil itself insofar as it is radical, while also contingent.

The function of exorcism is to "conjure" and expel the presence of that other-than-myself, to whom I yield whenever I sin, and who is the adversary of him who saves me. Because its point of application is the priority (in time) of evil to itself in man, exorcism is very logically a unilateral act of God with which the person is only passively associated. Only the minister exercises an active role by laying on his hand and pronouncing the adjuration. But this does not make the exorcism a sacrament, for it does not itself bring the catechumen to God, as baptism will bring him. It simply frees him from the "adversary", the center of iniquity, the non-human source of actual human evil.

[8] P. Ricoeur, *Finitude et culpabilité*, II: *La Symbolique du mal* (Paris, 1960), pp. 236-43, 289-320.

Emil Lengeling/*Wolbeck, West Germany*

Blessing of Baptismal Water in the Roman Rite

This article[1] is concerned with a paradox peculiar to the more recent practice of the Latin Church. Normally, baptismal water is blessed only on the Vigil of Easter[2] without baptism following the blessing; and when someone is baptized, the water is not blessed in the rite of baptism itself. On the other hand, Article 70 of the *Constitution on the Sacred Liturgy*[2a] declares: "Except during Eastertide,[3] baptismal water may be blessed within the rite of baptism itself by an approved shorter formula." The preparatory commission gave as reasons for this article the "squalid, unbecoming state of the water, often putrefying in the baptismal font" and the "integrity of catechesis and rite" which "is left somewhat obscure if it is

[1] Extensive illustrations from the sources and information about the abundant literature on the blessing of baptismal water can be found in E. Lengeling, *Die Taufwasserweihe der römischen Liturgie. Vorschlag nu einer Neuformung, Liturgie, Gestalt und Vollzug* (Munich: W. Dürig, 1963), pp. 176-251. To the bibliography there should be added J. de Jong, "Benedictio Fontis," in *Archiv für Lit. Wiss.* 8 (1963), pp. 21-46.

[2] Since the new order of Holy Week, this occurs no longer on the Vigil of Pentecost.

[2a] Subsequent references to the *Constitution on the Sacred Liturgy* will be indicated simply by the number of the Article.

[3] Two Council fathers wanted to replace in a *modus* the words *extra tempus paschale* by *extra Sabbatum Sanctum*. The commission rejected the *modus* because it would not do to use the water solemnly blessed only on the Easter Vigil. It is regrettable that just at Eastertide the most important reason for Article 70—the integration of the rite of baptism—is not brought into consideration. Evidently, the idea is still too deep-rooted that the blessing of water is a part of the Church's year and not of the rite of baptism.

completed only on the Easter Vigil with the magnificent exposition of the mystery of water".

Like all the sacraments, baptism not only presupposes, but nourishes, strengthens and signifies faith in word and rite, so that the faithful are empowered through the celebration "to receive this grace in a fruitful manner, to worship God duly and to practice charity" (n. 59). In the original conception of the Roman liturgy, together with the service of the Word on the Easter Vigil (and in Lent), the blessing of water (in the ancient form of the eucharistic-anamnetic prayer[4]) was meant to nourish faith and prepare for the operation of the Holy Spirit.[5] Since their detachment from this context, the prayers of the baptismal rite must now be described as theologically impoverished; they are in need of integration.[6]

In all the Eastern Churches and the Anglican Church the blessing of baptismal water has remained a necessary part of every administration of baptism.[7] It was the same in the Roman and the other Western rites, not only for baptism on the Easter Vigil (Leonine Sacramentary), but also at other times for baptism of the sick (still in some rituals in modern times) and,

[4] Cf. J.-P. Audet, *"Esquisse Historique du genre littéraire de la 'bénédiction' juive et de l' 'eucharistie' chrétienne,"* in *Rev. bibl.* 65 (1958), pp. 371-99.

[5] Cf. *Council of Trent, Decr. de iustificatione,* cap. 7 (DS 1529 [D799]).

[6] Certainly the quasi-mystagogic function can also be fulfilled through a prayer without blessing of water, as normally occurs in Protestant baptismal rites. In the renewed *ritus* such a prayer ought to be introduced for the occasions when someone is not allowed or does not want to bless the water. (Article 70 does not impose the obligation of blessing the water at every baptism.) But the place for such a prayer in all the ancient liturgies from early times is the blessing of the water.

[7] Brief petitions for the blessing of the water are also found in the baptismal rites of the Book of Common Order of the Church of Scotland (1940; London, 1963, p. 91), of the Book of Common Worship of the United Church of South India (1962; London, 1964, p. 108), of the Communauté Romande de travail liturgique (Lausanne, 1959, p. 12) and of the Reformed Church of Canton Vaud (*Liturgie*: Lausanne, 1964, p. 374). A blessing of baptismal water on the Easter Vigil with an altered Roman text is found in the altar book of the Old Catholics (Bonn, 1959, pp. 139f.), in K. B. Ritter (Michaelsbruderschaft) (Die euchar. Feier: Kassel, 1961, pp. 318ff.) and in Taizé (*Liturgies pascales,* 1962, pp. 58f.).

until late in the Middle Ages, for baptism of healthy children and adults.[8] Until the present day, at least in some dioceses, a frequent (weekly) blessing of water was required.

When the above-quoted Article 70 speaks of an approved shorter formula, it can scarcely be referring to the two formulas given in the Roman Ritual (Tit. II, cap. 8-9) when baptismal water has to be blessed again outside the Easter Vigil "because it has become corrupt, drained away or is simply not available" (Can. 757, §83). The first formula is much too long; the second is linked with an apostolic indult (given with decennial faculties in missionary countries, South America and the Philippines). Neither is "suitable":[9] the "mystery of water" is not expressed (cap. 9) or expressed only within an exorcism (cap. 8).

Since other texts of the Latin tradition outside the Easter Vigil are also scarcely suitable, it seems obvious to revert to the Easter Vigil. Thus the inner relationship of every baptism to the paschal mystery would be underlined in a desirable way. Certainly, text and rite would have to be shortened and simplified in the sense of the *Constitution on the Sacred Liturgy*[10] and indeed for use also on the Easter Vigil.

In spite of its age[11] and its beauty, the Roman blessing of water presents serious defects in text and rite:

1. The *text* contains:

(a) Elements utterly heterogeneous in matter and style, which do not smoothly follow one another and which partly repeat themselves.

(b) Some sentences in the exorcisms and in the section *Respice* (*conceptio, uterus*) are scarcely or not at all suitable for modern languages. Baptism by immersion is presupposed twice, although it is no longer used. Addressing the water also raises misgivings.

[8] Cf. also St. Thomas, *Summa Theologica* III, q. 66 a. 3 ad 5.
[9] In the draft there stood, instead of *probata, apta*.
[10] Cf. Arts. 21, 23, 24, 33, 34, 62.
[11] The modern text (without the formulas for the pouring of oil) is already in the old Gelasian Sacramentary, which was written about 750 in Gaul. Some parts are much older. It is disputed whether the text is purely Roman or whether it contains additions from Ravenna or Gaul.

(c) In the series of paradigms, the most important New Testament (cf. 1 Cor. 10, 13) and patristic, specifically paschal, type is lacking: namely, the passage through the Red Sea, which in other (also Western) rites has a place of honor.

(d) The image of rebirth is developed one-sidedly from the theology of baptism. There is lacking (as in the rest of the Roman baptismal rite, by contrast with other liturgies in East and West) the Pauline teaching[12] that "by baptism men are plunged into the paschal mystery of Christ" (n. 6; cf. n. 109).

2. Regarding the *rite:*

(a) The incorporated formulas of exorcisms and blessing, as well as the conclusion typical for exorcisms,[13] are in no way suited to the literary genre of a consecratory prayer such as we also find in the other great consecratory prefaces.

(b) While the old Gelasian Sacramentary provides only for a sign of the cross (at the *Spiritus sancti*), from the 9th to the 16th centuries the joyful medieval attitude led to a steadily mounting increase in the number of rites. This ritual structure cannot be said to have been of "noble simplicity . . . short, clear and unencumbered by useless repetitions . . . within the people's powers of comprehension, and normally should not require much explanation" (n. 34).

(c) The pouring of chrism has migrated from the Gallic to the Gelasian use of the 8th century, but it was not taken up in all areas of the Roman rite until the Roman Missal of 1570. Since the 10th century, in some places a mixture of chrism and oil of catechumens has been poured in. The present pouring in three stages exists only since 1570. There has never been any attempt to bring it into organic unity with the consecratory prayer. While the mixing of chrism was regarded in Gaul (and in the East) as constitutive, the Roman view is that the blessing is effected through the prayer.

(d) The dipping of the Easter candle is not ancient Gallic, but can be shown to have appeared only about 800 in certain

[12] Rom. 6, 1-12; Eph. 2, 5-6; Col. 2, 12-13; 3, 1; 2 Tim. 2, 11.

[13] The section *Unde benedico* also was originally—as it is still today in the Roman Ritual (II, 8) and in Milan—an exorcism.

places in the Frankish and South German areas. The rite gradually penetrated the Roman books through the influence of the Romano-German pontifical (Mainz, about 950), but was not accepted everywhere until modern times, indeed, up to the 19th century—in Rome certainly only after the exile at Avignon.[14] Up to the present time it has not been found in the rites of Milan, Toledo, Braga and Lyons. The rite and the sung epiclesis for the descent of the Spirit originally had nothing to do with one another; the Easter candle is in fact a symbol of Christ.[15]

Because of the deficiencies only briefly outlined here, a revised consecratory prayer, both for the Easter Vigil and for baptism at other times, in the spirit of the *Constitution on the Sacred Liturgy,* might "in some way grow organically" (n. 23) out of the traditional text. The introductory prayer ought to remain.[16] The consecratory prayer itself should not contain any exorcism. If the latter, in accordance with the oldest tradition of all liturgies (apart from those of the Reformers and Old Catholics), is to remain—and this can certainly be justified theologically[17]—the laws of liturgical form would require it to be placed before the consecratory prayer. But a formula with an address to the devil (*Exorcizo te*) is not desirable; instead (as in Eastern blessings of baptismal water), there ought to be a prayer. With a little alteration, the section *Procul—consequantur* of the present preface suggests itself.

Adapting the traditional text, the consecratory prayer might run somewhat like this:[18]

[14] In the Roman rite (not in all sources) the acolytes' candles were put into the water at the beginning of the blessing and remained there until after baptism.

[15] Simply because text and rite originally had nothing to do with one another, it is impossible to maintain the frequently asserted phallic meaning of the rite, for which the text provides an occasion.

[16] In this respect, we must reflect whether the original textual forms are to be restored in every case.

[17] Cf. Gen. 3, 17; Jn. 12, 31; 14, 30; 16, 11; Rom. 8, 20-22; 2 Cor. 4, 4; 1 Jn. 5, 19.

[18] Compared with the Latin text, which I presented for discussion in 1963 (cf. *supra,* footnote 1), the present text—at least so I hope—shows some improvements which I owe partially to discussions with specialist colleagues.

O God, your Spirit moved at the beginning of the world over the waters, so that they might even then receive the power to sanctify. In the waters of the flood you then signified rebirth, since the same element meant death for the sinner and life for the just. You made Abraham's children pass dry-shod over the Red Sea, in order that the people freed from Egyptian servitude might prefigure the sacrament of your Church. In the waters of the Jordan your Son chose to be baptized by John. Hanging on the cross, together with his blood, he also made water spring from his side. He commanded his disciples to baptize in water those who believed, saying: "Go: make disciples of all nations, baptizing them in the name of the Father and the Son and the Holy Spirit."

Graciously look down then, O Lord, on your Church and open to her this font of baptism. Let it be a living font, a water of purification and rebirth. Let it receive the grace of your only-begotten Son from the Holy Spirit, so that man, created in your image, washed free from all ancient stain in the sacrament of baptism, by water and the Holy Spirit may be reborn to new sonship.

(*At the dipping of the Easter candle*): May there descend upon this water, we beg you, the Spirit of your Son, so that those who are buried in baptism with Christ unto his death may rise with him to life. Through him, our Lord Jesus Christ. . . .

The suggested text ought to correspond to the special genre of all great consecratory prayers. Before the petition and the epiclesis, in accordance with the intentions of Article 70 of the *Constitution on the Sacred Liturgy*, we must recall the most important salvation-historical paradigms: creation, flood, passage through the Red Sea (new), baptism of Christ, water from his side. It is true that we are abandoning the form of a preface. This has gradually prevailed (not in the Ambrosian and Mozarabic rites) only since the 8th century, as the result of a misunderstood rubric (to be sung in the tone of the preface). Neverthe-

less, as in the Canon of the Mass, the anamnesis is always implicitly a thanksgiving. The command to baptize leads to the
petition that God may sanctify the water to serve rebirth.

The theology of baptism as dying and rising with Christ is
illustrated by a single dipping of the Easter candle,[19] which
symbolizes Christ. The text of the epiclesis of the Spirit is
adapted to the rite: it is the Holy Spirit proceeding from Christ
who is invoked. The pouring of oil (never integrated in the
liturgy) is omitted: (1) because the prayer for the blessing is
constitutive; (2) so that the impression of dipping the candle
is not weakened (a rite that no one would want to abandon);
(3) for hygienic reasons. Moreover, omitting the oil facilitates
a desirable clarification of the central sacramental sign: baptism
in "living", running water and a baptism by immersion.[20]

In the rite of baptism the blessing of water would not have
to be inserted (as is customary only in Rome and Milan) between the renunciations and the profession of faith, since these
acts, according to the oldest and (apart from Rome and Milan)
universal tradition, are complementary; nor—as today in the
Eastern rites—after the act of faith, since this is in the closest
relationship to the center of the *sacramentum fidei;* but, as in the
other Western orders of baptism until modern times (also in
what was formerly the Roman rite), before the renunciations.[21]

[19] Repetition and gradation developed here and there toward the end
of the Middle Ages. The present form has been in the Roman Missal
only since 1570.

[20] Cf. Jn. 14, 10; Num. 20, 6f.; Jer. 2, 13; Zech. 14, 8 and the apt
observation of St. Thomas Aquinas (*Summa Theologica* I, q. 18, a. 1,
ad 3); for concrete suggestions, cf. the review *L'Art Sacré* 5/6, 1963
and 5/6, 1966. In some of Munich's new churches, baptismal fonts with
running water have been installed.

[21] As far as the arrangements for the blessing of water on the Easter
Vigil are concerned, the absurd position—after baptism or the renewal
of baptismal promises—given in the most recent reform to the responsory *Sicut cervus* and the following prayer will have to be changed
again. The blessing of water in a substitute font, introduced at that time,
contradicts the text of the blessing. The water should be blessed in the
real baptismal font. But this ought to be within sight of the faithful. Cf.
L'Art Sacré, loc. cit.; E. E. Gloff, *Liturgie und Kirchenraum* (Zurich,
1964), pp. 43-53; A.-M. Roguet, *Construire et aménager les églises*
(Paris, 1965), pp. 79-92.

Joseph Gelineau, S.J./*Paris, France*

The Chants of the Baptismal Liturgy

According to the present Roman rite, the celebration of the sacrament of baptism does not involve any singing. The absence of this normal accompaniment to festal and communitarian worship is a consequence of the historical evolution through which the sacrament of baptism has passed. As a result of this process, by baptism we have come to mean almost exclusively the baptisms of children celebrated individually. As a result, baptism has now come to possess that family character—somewhat intimate and private, one might almost say—with which we have grown so familiar.

Yet, considered as a rite of transition, as a paschal celebration and as the means of entry into the community of believers, Christian baptism is a supreme "festal" occasion, and the normal way to express our feelings on such an occasion is by singing together. If the renewal of the celebration of the eucharist has, along with the active participation of the faithful, brought with it the renewal of singing in our assemblies, surely baptism, which is a much rarer "feast" and a truly privileged moment in the life of a community, also calls for the restoration of singing as a means of demonstrating the full meaning of the sacrament. In addition, might not singing be instrumental in giving the whole People of God a quite new and profound understanding of the true meaning of this sacrament?

Of course, there is nothing new in this suggestion. Even a cursory examination of tradition and comparative liturgy proves that there has always been much singing of various kinds in the Christian baptismal liturgy, but this is not widely known. Therefore, at a time when the need for baptismal chants is increasingly being appreciated, it is only right that we should devote our attention to this whole matter. First of all, then, we shall quite briefly examine the facts as they appear in tradition, quoting, by way of illustration, the principal chants used in the different liturgies. We shall then go on to discuss how singing should or could play its part in a restored order of the baptismal rites.

In keeping with the main theme of this volume, we shall confine our consideration of the problem to the aspect of the sacrament as administered to adults. This, of course, cannot be restricted merely to the actual baptismal ceremony. It embraces the whole preparation of the catechumenate and has a particular place in the liturgy of Lent, Holy Week, the Easter Vigil and the octave of "renewal", and it is a fact that all these celebrations have baptismal chants intimately associated with them.

I

BAPTISMAL CHANTS ACCORDING TO THE EVIDENCE OF COMPARATIVE LITURGY

The baptismal chants found in the rituals, *ordines* or *typica* offer us the whole range of expression, forms and types of chant that are used in Christian worship. Here we find acclamations, dialogues and litanies, psalms, troparia and antiphons, and many kinds of hymns. We shall now examine each of these according to their different categories.

1. *Acclamations, Dialogues and Litanies*

The way in which we show that the whole community is sharing in a sacred action depends, in the first place, on the parts of the celebration that are given over to acclamations, dialogues and litanies; for it is by joining in these that the people as a whole become actors in the drama of the mystery, as they ratify and reply to what is being said and raise their voices in supplication and thanksgiving. Here we find the *cardo* of the action and that which ultimately determines the whole *tonus* of the festivity. Replies and responses made only by a *ministrans* are totally inadequate, and words alone are not sufficient. To ensure that the people are truly actors in the celebration we must have the singing of the whole assembly.

This is especially true of the responses made by the people to the invitations of the celebrant before the prayers and the *Amens* with which the prayers conclude, in addition to the more highly developed dialogues that form the introductions to prefaces such as the blessing of the water.

But the rituals also contain many other examples of acclamations whose purpose is to maintain the assembly in a state of active participation. For example, the Maronite preface for the blessing of water is continually punctuated with responses made by the people, such as: *To you, God of Abraham, God of Isaac, God of Jacob, King glorious and holy forever* (Dz 343).[1] In the Egyptian rites, we find the same preface continuing into a *Sanctus* (As 169). According to the *ordo* of Constantinople, the celebrant sings the *alleluia* three times with the people as he pours the oil into the font (As 141). In the liturgy of the Western Syrians, the trinitarian formula which accompanies the triple immersion is given particular prominence by the addition of the three Amens: *This man is baptized in the name of the Father—AMEN—and of the Son—AMEN—and of the Holy Spirit forever—AMEN* (Dz 374).

Under the general heading of litanies we also group together

[1] So as not to burden this article with complicated notes, for the rituals we shall refer to the two best known collections, the letters indicating the work, and the numerals the page:

As = J. Assemani, *Codex Liturgicus Ecclesiae Universae* II: *De Baptismo* (Rome, 1749).

Dz = H. Denzinger, *Ritus Orientalium* I (Wurzburg, 1863; Graz, 1961).

all those prayers made up of a series of intentions delivered by a deacon or by cantors to which the people reply by some invocation. Examples of this type abound in the baptismal rituals, and may conveniently be divided into two kinds.

The first is by far the most important. It consists essentially of prayers offered by the deacon for the catechumens to which the people reply with an invocation, such as the *Kyrie eleison*. We find these prayers either at the beginning of the rite (e.g., As 131), or, as is more usually the case, at the end of the "liturgy of the Word" (e.g., As 157).

The second kind, which is particularly characteristic of the West, can be described as a processional litany, and we can see a highly developed example of this at the Easter Vigil celebration in the Roman rite. According to the Gelasian *ordo,* there were three of this type of litany, each undoubtedly embodying the *Kyrie eleison, invocations to the saints and the Agnus Dei.* On the evidence of the *Ordines,* it would seem that each movement from place to place was accompanied by a litany. During the Middle Ages they underwent important developments and became a highly organized affair. According to circumstances, the various ministers would repeat each invocation seven, five, four or three times (e.g., As 90). But whatever its type, it is true to say that the litany still remains the privileged form of communal prayer.

2. *The Psalms*

In the baptismal rites, just as in the rest of the liturgy, extensive use is made of psalms. Here they fulfill different functions, and to these functions there are correspondingly suitable psalmodic forms. An examination of the principal examples can be most instructive. In the first place we must mention the *responsorial psalm* which we find placed between the readings in every instance of a "liturgy of the Word". For this purpose the following psalms are the ones most frequently used:[2]

Psalm 26 (*The Lord is my light and my help*), the prayer

---

[2] The psalms are referred to according to their liturgical numbering (LXX).

of hope on the lips of the catechumen during his pre-baptismal combat (e.g., the second *prokeimenon* of Easter night at Constantinople).[3]

Psalm 28, which is the text most frequently used because of the wording of v. 3 (*The Lord's voice resounding on the waters*).

Psalm 22 (*The Lord is my shepherd*), which has been used from the time of the patristic catechesis to signify the sacraments of Christian initiation (e.g., the Armenian ritual, As 196).

Psalm 113 or the Easter psalm, illustrating the spiritual exodus of baptism and the salvation that comes through the water (e.g., Dz 282).

The Canticle of Moses (Exodus 15), which is traditional on the Easter Vigil, etc.

Secondly, we find psalms used as chants accompanying a particular rite because of the fact that its text provides an apt description of the meaning of the rite. Two celebrated examples of this immediately spring to mind.

In the Western (Roman, Milanese, Mozarabic) tradition, the procession of the *baptizandi* to the font takes place to the accompaniment of the singing of Psalm 41: *Sicut cervus desiderat ad fontes.*[4] It is most surprising to find no trace of the use of this psalm in the East.

Then in the Byzantine tradition—no doubt of Palestinian origin—Psalm 31, or the psalm of pardon (*Happy the man whose offense is forgiven*) is solemnly chanted immediately after the immersion. According to the Tipicon of Constantinople, on the Vigils of Easter and the Epiphany, as the neophytes return in procession from the baptistery, the deacon sings the verses at the ambo, and all take up "Happy the man. . . ."[5] According

---

[3] J. Mateos, *Le Tipicon de la Grand Eglise* II (*Orient. Christ. Anal.* 165-166) (Rome, 1962), p. 85.

[4] St. Jerome in *Adv. Pel.* III, 15 (*P.L.* 23, 585) quite clearly quotes this psalm for this very same moment of the rite. Cf. Cyril of Jerusalem, *1st Baptismal Catechesis* (*P.G.* 33, 369); Gregory of Nazianzen, *Sermon on Baptism*, n. 30.

[5] J. Mateos, *op. cit.* II, p. 91. Cf. *ibid.*, I, p. 185, "The Vigil of the Epiphany" during the post-baptismal anointing by the bishop and then during the procession.

to the *ordo baptismalis* of the Euchologion of Venice (As 145), the priest sings with the people.[6]

Thirdly, very many individual psalm verses are to be found on their own combined with troparia in chants we shall discuss later on. It is interesting to note that the texts used in this way are nearly always the same: Pss. 28, 3; 76, 17-18; 113, 5; 33, 6; 44, 8; 65, 13; 131, 13, etc. For the blessing of the water, the Alexandrian ritual even includes a chant that is made up out of a series of such verses punctuated with alleluias (As 178).

Finally, there are psalms used as a preparation for the celebration, either in the manner of Pss. 8, 21 and 41 which are indicated in the Roman ritual at the beginning of the baptism of adults, or for the entry into the Church, such as Psalm 50 (with intercalated troparia) in the Syrian, Armenian and Alexandrian rites.

There are two points which emerge from this brief summary: first, the convergence of tradition around six or seven "baptismal" psalms, and, secondly, the variety of ways in which they are used in chants of various forms, many performing different functions.

3. *The Troparia*

In addition to the inspired psalms, there are two other types of chants found in the baptismal rites: namely, troparia and hymns.

The troparia—with which the extended Latin *antiphonae* and the Syrian *onyata* are connected—occupy a special place in the tradition of liturgical song. The text, varying in length and usually in prose, forcefully and vividly expresses the mystery which is celebrated in a biblical language, but it does not necessarily keep close to the letter of scripture.[7] It is usually

---

[6] Compare the Ordo of the Western Syrians (Dz 277): three times by the assistants. In the Alexandrian Ordo, Psalm 31 is sung between the readings, before the gospel (As 154). On the other hand, Psalm 33 is used as a post-baptismal chant by the Armenians and the Western Syrians (As 201; Dz 376).

[7] Cf. D. Rimaud, "Le genre littéraire du tropaire," in *Eglise qui chante*, 71-72. (Paris: June, 1966), pp. 46-49.

combined with one or more carefully chosen verses of a psalm and the *Gloria Patri,* and sung to music, which closely follows the words, either by cantors or by the people as a whole or in part. The troparia provide the principal lyrical highlights of the celebration, as can be seen from the following examples.

The most important of the baptismal troparia is the text of Galatians 3, 27: *Omnes qui in Christo baptizati estis, Christus induistis.* It is found as an entry chant in the Easter Vigil Mass in the Chaldean rite, and in the Masses of the Epiphany and of Pentecost in the Mozarabic rite. In the Byzantine rite, it is sung in place of the Trisagion (the ancient entry chant), commencing with the sixth Sunday of Lent (Lazarus). During Easter night it is sung between the readings from the Old Testament and those from St. Paul. It thus appears at the actual time of the baptism,[8] and reads as follows (with a *responsio a latere*):

All you who have been baptized into Christ,
You have put on Christ. Alleluia. (*three times*)
V. Gloria Patri. . . . Nunc et semper. . . .
R. You have put on Christ. Alleluia.
All you. . . .

The connection between this troparion and the central act of the sacrament emerges clearly from the examination of those interrelated rituals in which it has been preserved.[9] In the Armenian rite, it comes after the immersion, but in more developed form (As 201):

You who have been baptized into Christ,
You have put on Christ. Alleluia.
You who have been enlightened in the Father,
In you the Holy Spirit will rejoice. Alleluia.

[8] J. Mateos, *Le Tipicon* . . . II, p. 91.
[9] This chant appears to be so important that in the Byzantine Ordo, even for the baptism of a child in danger of death, the priest must take the baptized child in his arms and sing this troparion (As 148).

In the Chaldean rite, it appears with further poetic elaboration:[10]

You who have been baptized into Christ,
You have put on Christ, through the water and through the
    Spirit,
To reign with him in the abode of heaven.

The rituals also highlight other moments in the baptism by using chants that we can classify as troparia; often they are models of liturgical literature and prayer.

In the Western Syrian rites, at the moment of the immersion, the deacons, using the tone of St. Balai,[11] sing:

Descend, O brethren marked with the seal,
And put on [Christ] our Lord:
Become yourselves a part of his noble race,
As it is spoken in his parable.

And as the baptized come out of the bath, it continues with other verses full of bold imagery:

Stretch out your wings, O holy Church,
And greet the simple lambs
Whom the Holy Spirit has begotten from the waters. . . .

For the reception of the "garment of justice", the Ordo of Constantinople gives the following beautiful troparion (As 146):

Bestow upon me the shining tunic,
You who are clothed with light as with a mantle,
Most merciful Christ, our God.

[10] Onita d-qankē of the Easter Mass and of the mawtba of the Epiphany. Cf. J. Mateos, Lelya-Sapra, Essai d'interprétation des matines chaldéeanes (Orient. christ. Anal. 156) (Rome, 1959), p. 135, n. 3.

[11] The Ordo of James of Edessa according to Bar Hebraeus (Ds 287). Cf. other ordines, ibid., pp. 294, 307. The pentasyllabic chants (Balaic chants) are associated with the name of Balai, an episcopal hymnographer at the beginning of the 5th century.

As an equivalent to the Latin *Sicut cervus* during the procession to the baptistery, in the patriarchal liturgy of Constantinople the psalmists sing this song:

The voice of the Lord cries out over the waters, saying:
Come, all of you, and receive the Spirit of wisdom, the Spirit
    of understanding,
The Spirit of fear of God, from him who has appeared.

In the Alexandrian ritual, after the five readings, a response follows the gospel of Nicodemus expressing the prayer and faith of the baptized:[12]

We believe in you, O our Master:
Enlighten our eyes and pour out the light into our hearts,
So that we may become the sons of light.

However, the baptismal liturgy is not confined to the final rites of the sacrament. It also includes the preparation of the catechumenate during Lent and the whole of the Easter week of renewal. In spite of the complete disappearance of the ancient baptismal discipline, scattered traces of it are to be found in practically all the liturgies. It is here that we find the most beautiful of the texts used in the baptismal chants.

In the Chaldean rite, at *Sapra* (the morning office) during the first five days of Holy Week, there still remains a procession to the baptistery.[13] Some of the processional *onyata* sung on this occasion are particularly fine. This one, for Holy Thursday, is obviously addressed to the catechumens:

The doors of the chamber of the spiritual nuptials are open
    for the pardon of men,
And here it is that, with the gift of the heavenly Spirit,
Mercy and clemency are bestowed upon all.

[12] J. Mateos, *Le Tipicon* . . . I, p. 183. The subject is the baptisms celebrated on the Vigil of the Epiphany.
[13] J. Mateos, *Lelva-Sapra*, p. 204.

Even now, O invited guests, enter into the joy which has been
    prepared for you,
And with a pure and holy heart, with true faith,
Give thanks to Christ, our Lord.

The troparion sung on Holy Thursday is a truly wonderful
catechesis:

It is not from the well of Jacob,
Nor from the waters made sweet by Moses,
Nor from the river of the Jordan
Which was sanctified by your baptism at the hand of John,
But it is from your side, O Christ,
That springs the source of life
Through which our debts are forgiven
And our sins cleansed away.

The *onyatas* of the office of Easter night are even more poetic
and lyrical, while still retaining the same density of meaning:[14]

O guests invited to the banquet of the Son, the deliverer of the
    universe,
O men who were dead and from error have been called to
    life,
Purify yourselves in the blood of the Son, the King.
O firstborn, sons of the Church, see, in the mystery,
The glory of the Son who has summoned you to the light from
    on high.
The love from on high has come down and has given us life.

Certain pieces in the Byzantine liturgy could have received
their basic inspiration from the sacrament of baptism, as, for
instance, this *kondakion* still preserved on the sixth Sunday
after Easter (the man born blind):

[14] *Ibid.*, p. 229. Compare the series of the *mawtba* of the Epiphany,
p. 135, which seems to have the same origin.

Blind in the eyes of the soul, I draw near to you, O Christ,
As the man born blind, crying out to you in my repentance:
"Thou art the resplendent light for those who are in darkness."

Neither is this type of chant absent from the Roman liturgy. Although they are of a more literally scriptural style, the three gospel communion antiphons for the three ancient scrutiny Masses (the Samaritan woman: *Qui biberit;* the man born blind: *Lutum fecit;* Lazarus: *Videns Dominus*), which are still sung to melodies of a quite distinctive simplicity, are examples of baptismal troparia which at the same time are also eucharistic.

4. *The Hymns*

The hymn, especially the hymn written in regular strophic poetry, has always provided the greatest opportunity for the people to express themselves in song. Therefore, before closing our summary of the baptismal chants as found in tradition, it is important that this type of popular song should be given our close attention.

The most ancient Christian baptismal hymn is to be found in Ephesians 5, 14;

Awake, O sleeper, and arise from the dead,
And Christ shall give you light.

From a quotation by Clement of Alexandria we know how this hymn continued:

Light of the resurrection,
Begotten before the morning star
Who gives life through his radiance.

However, this venerable piece does not appear in any of the ancient baptismal rituals.

It must be said that the Latin West is extremely poor in baptismal hymnody, both in quantity and quality. A ritual originating from Poitiers has preserved a *Versus* (a hymn with a refrain in uniform verses) written by Fortunatus: *Tibi laus perennis auctor, Baptismatis sacrator* (As 60). It is the exact counterpart of the *O Redemptor, sume carmen* still used for the consecration of the holy oils on Holy Thursday. The final verse of this hymn is well worth quoting:

> Gaudete candidati,
> Electa vasa regni,
> In morte consepulti,
> Christi fide renati.

Nor is the Byzantine world any richer in this respect. It was in the Syrian tradition that this type of song particularly flourished.[15] And here Ephraem, the creator of the *midrasha* (a poetic form of preaching in uniform verses, concluding with a refrain for the people) still stands head and shoulders above all others as the great creative genius. His nine baptismal hymns are a monument of poetic, scriptural and sacramental theology, a veritable mystagogy, where we find explained not only the *mysteria* of the rites, but also natural symbols and biblical imagery.[16] Here is a verse from the seventh hymn illustrating the sign of the bath (verse 15):

> A weary body is bathed in the water and rests from its labor;
> Here is the bath where rest, life and delights lie hidden;
> There rests an exhausted Adam, who introduced weariness into the creation.

The Syrian baptismal rituals also contain an appreciable number of hymns written in the same vein. Thus, before the liturgy of the Word we find a *qolo* composed by *Ququoio* (a

[15] We can also mention many of the *Odes of Solomon* originating in Jewish-Christian circles, where the baptismal inspiration is quite evident (e.g., Odes 9 and 15).

[16] These are the "Hymns of the Epiphany"; cf. *Hymnes de l'Epiphanie*, ed. E. Beck (*Corp. Script. Christ. Orient.*, 186). German translation: n. 187, pp. 131ff.).

deacon hymnographer of the 5th to the 6th centuries) which in very simple language sets out the whole mystery of baptism.[17] During the pre-baptismal anointing, a hymn is sung celebrating the mystery of the holy oil.[18] Finally, a long hymn of thanksgiving brings the baptism to a close ("while they put on their garments" is the rubric in the Maronite Ordo); this was also used as a communion chant:[19]

> My brethren, sing glory to the Son of the Lord of the universe,
> Who has fashioned for you a crown that kings would envy.
> Your garments, brethren, have the brightness of the sun,
> And your countenances shine like those of the angels.
> The fruit that Adam could not taste in paradise
> Is today, in gladness, pressed upon your lips. . . .
> You have received the bliss of heaven:
> Watch, lest the Evil One snatch it from you. . . .
> Go in peace, children of the baptism:
> Adore the cross which will watch over you.

II

THE BAPTISMAL CHANTS IN A RESTORED LITURGY

The conciliar *Constitution on the Sacred Liturgy* foresees, on the one hand, the rearrangement of the rites of adult baptism along with the restoration of the catechumenate (Art. 66), and, on the other, the reorganization of those features of Lent which are especially concerned with baptism (Art. 109). Both of these reforms involve the restoration of singing in the assemblies, where both the catechumens and the faithful will be

[17] *Joannes misquit aquas baptismatis* . . . (Dz 284). Cf. various other verses, pp. 270, 293, 310-11.

[18] *Oleo sancto edixit Deus* . . . (Dz 286). Compare pp. 277, 294, 307 and 314. Here we must mention Ephraem's three madrashim on the sacrament of the oil, *Hymni de Virginitate*, ed. I. Rahmani (Charfé, 1906); Latin translation, pp. 10-21.

[19] Dz 288; also cf. 301 and 349. Compare with this the *Hymnum novelli christiani* which concludes the Ethiopian Ordo of Alexandria (Dz 233).

able to celebrate together, as a community, all the various stages of the sacrament, sometimes on separate occasions and at other times within a Sunday Mass.

While we are as yet unable to describe these chants in detail before the reforms of the *Ordo baptismi* and the Lenten Lectionary are promulgated, it is still possible for us to give a general indication, according to their various categories, of the type of chants that will most certainly be needed, and of those that would be desirable or possible.

1. *Responsorial Psalms in the Liturgies of the Word*

Most of the meetings that concern the catechumenate will undoubtedly take place in the framework of a "liturgy of the Word", either separately (the entry to the catechumenate, the minor exorcisms, election, scrutinies and traditions), or be included in the first part of a Lenten Mass (e.g., the scrutiny Masses). The baptism itself will eventually, as foreseen, once more include this basic and constituent feature of Christian worship.

Every liturgy of the Word normally includes, after the first reading, an actual psalm, sung if possible in responsorial form. The choice of this psalm will depend, first of all, on the reading that precedes it, but also on the purpose of the *synaxis*. The greatest care will have to be exercised in choosing not only the psalm, but also the verse intended to serve as a "response" (refrain) for the people. For both of these choices most valuable pointers and suggestions are provided by the ancient lectionaries. In many cases, the responsorial psalm could be the psalm used for all the chants throughout the synaxis.

2. *The Litanies*

Every synaxis includes a prayer of intercession for the catechumens—distinct from the *Oratio fidelium,* if this subsequently follows—concluding with a prayer by the celebrant. The most natural form of this prayer is the diaconal litany with invocations sung by the assembly. Although the *Kyrie eleison* will always remain a model of such invocations, they could, with profit, be varied according to the particular nature of the prayer: *Adjuva nos, Domine, Libera nos, Domine,* etc.

Processional litanies of the Western type could be used for movements from place to place. However, long series of invocations to the saints are not always necessary. In fact, there are many who would even like to see their reduction in the Easter Vigil liturgy (especially in the absence of any real procession).

3. *The Acclamations*

We presuppose that the dialogues between the celebrant and the people or between the deacon and the people, as well as the conclusions of the prayers, will be sung every time that the nature of the assembly and the style of the celebration permit. After all, here we have the primary element of any expression of communitarian and festive worship. However, according to the nature of the rites and the particular genius of the various peoples, we must also envisage the possibility of their singing other collective interventions (as, for instance, the renewal of the baptismal promise by the community). In fact, in the liturgy of the Easter Vigil, when only a speaking voice is used for the responses made together ("We do renounce them" and "We do believe"), their effectiveness is often lost and can result in a complete break in the style of the celebration. It is also to be desired that prefaces such as that for the blessing of the water should either have the acclamations of the people integrated into them as an essential part, or at least should lead up to a *confessio* in which all take part.

4. *The Hymn before the Gospel*

In the liturgy of the Word, after the assembly has listened to the readings and the homily, and before passing on to the prayers, there is a need for some opportunity to meditate upon the Word and to assimilate it in an active and communitarian fashion in lyrical form, thus transforming it into a *confessio* or *deprecatio,* and eventually preparing for the rite to follow.

The value of such a chant, which we can discuss although it might not be imposed, is evident from a number of considerations:

(a) As we have said, the need to assimilate the Word.

(b) The desire expressed by communities, where the catechumens are dismissed after the prayers offered up on their behalf, for a celebration which will be of a sufficiently warmhearted, comprehensive and festive nature (e.g., in Africa, where catechumens could not be brought together merely for a ceremony lasting only twenty minutes).

(c) The pastoral benefits that accrue from popular hymn singing. For this the responsorial psalm is not sufficient. Just as the scriptural lesson is brought to life in the homily, so a hymn serves to express the faith and the prayer of the community in its own religious, poetical and musical language.

(d) If a catechumenal rite is to follow (the handing over of the gospel, inscription of the name, tradition, etc.), such a chant constitutes a link between the Word and the rite. It is both a preparation for and a mystagogy of the rite.

Undoubtedly, hymns of this kind will have to be worked out or composed in every language and for each type of synaxis, since what is to be done for the prayers surely should also be done for the singing.[20]

5. *The Entry Chants*

The opening of a synaxis normally, though not necessarily nor in every case, calls for an entry chant leading to a prayer. The purpose of this chant is twofold: to knit the community

[20] In tradition, that which corresponds to this type of chant is most usually found before or between the readings (troparia, qale, responses, proses and sequences). But experience shows that at the present time it is not advisable to draw out the entry rites of a synaxis (a chant and a prayer are sufficient), nor to separate the readings except by the natural connecting link of the responsorial psalm and the acclamation replying to the gospel. An excellent study by B. Huijbers on "Le chant après l'évangile" will be found in *Musique sacrée et langue modernes* (Coll. Kinnor, 4) (Paris, 1964), pp. 77ff., as well as examples of Dutch hymn compositions that are relevant here.

together and to introduce it into the mystery to be celebrated. For this chant either troparia with a refrain and versicles or a hymn with a refrain could be used.[21]

For synaxes of a clearly defined nature and purpose, individual texts will have to be composed. This will be true, for example, in the case of the Lenten scrutiny Masses where the tone is already set by the readings used.[22]

6. *Chants Accompanying Certain Special Rites*

Through a study of the rituals we have seen that certain rites such as the processions, the pre-baptismal anointings and the immersion itself used to be accompanied by, or set in the framework of, chants adapted for the purpose. There are many different reasons of both a ritualistic and practical nature for such chants:

(a) To keep the community active during a long rite (important movements from place to place, inscriptions of names, long series of exorcisms, handing over of the gospels, etc.).

(b) To serve as the mystagogy of a special rite (the signing

[21] On the nature and the adaptation to the entry chant of these two classifications, see J. Gelineau, *Les chants processionnaux* (*Eglise qui chante* 71-72): "Le chant d'entrée," pp. 8-20.

[22] A number of suggested texts have been presented to the Centre national de Pastorale liturgique (CNPL) de France which has given us permission to quote one as an example. Here is a suggested text for an entry chant for the third scrutiny Mass (Lazarus):

Verse:

Le maitre de la vie s' approche du tombeau:
"Lazare, éveille-toi d'entre les morts!
Et vous, ensevelis dans le péché,
Voyez et croyez que je suis le résurrection."

Refrain:

Si nous mourons avec toi, Seigneur,
Avec toi, nous entrerons dans la vie.

Versicles: Ps. 29, vv. 2, 3, 6b, 13; 1 Cor 11, 16.

An international commission devoted to research on the texts of troparia and hymns has been set up within the Association "Universa Laus" (an international study group for singing and music in the liturgy), which will gladly receive suggestions and collaboration in this work. (Address: Universa Laus, CP 78, 1950, Sion Suisse).

with the cross, the imposition of the name, the ephpheta, the anointing, the bestowal of the new garment or candle, etc.).

(c) To furnish a lyrical climax or turning point at a particularly important moment in the celebration (e.g., at the end of the triple bath).

Here it will be sufficient to mention an example of each case. At the time of the entry to the catechumenate, when the candidates are solemnly introduced into the church, it is fitting that the community should welcome them with song. A suggestion for this would be certain verses of Psalm 33—for example, verses 4, 6 and 13 with the refrain:

Come, my sons, listen to me,
That I might teach you the fear of the Lord.

The closing three rites of the baptism (the anointing, clothing and the candle) could very well be given added emphasis by the community through the singing of a troparion or of three suitable verses of a hymn or similar music after each formula of the rite.[23]

Finally, when the sacramental bath takes place, at this solemn moment one would like to see the whole community raise its voice in some song such as the traditional troparion:

[23] Thus a French baptismal canticle (*Source vive*, I, 49), with the text written by a well-known poet, comprises three verses which we may quote as an example:

Huile sainte, onction du salut,
Imprègne-moi, embaume-moi
De l'Esprit du Christ, Prêtre et Roi
Qui m'incorpore au peuple élu.

Drape moi, linge neuf et blanc,
De Jésus-Christ ressuscité;
Qu'avec toi, vêtu de clarté,
Je vienne au jour du jugement.

Cierge d'or, Feu qui purifie,
Consume en moi l'ombre et la mort
Et conduis mon âme et mon corps
A la lumière et à la vie.

All you who have been baptized into Christ,
You have put on Christ. Alleluia, alleluia!

7. *The Final Hymn*

Often an ordinary synaxis is brought to a close by a prayer of dismissal or blessing. Sometimes, if the eucharist of the faithful does not subsequently follow, it would be appropriate to round off the synaxis with a chant in which all take part. For this it would be easy to make use of well-known selections adapted for the occasion, but of a less specialized nature.

However, the actual celebration of the baptism will call not only for a special communion chant for the eucharist,[24] but also for a final hymn of praise and thanksgiving, many beautiful examples of which we have quoted above.

The liturgical reform of baptism—and of the other sacraments—called for by the Council clearly requires not only an extensive renewal of the singing of the Christian assemblies, but also a range of hymnody that will express the meaning of the mysteries to be celebrated and be adapted to the particular genius of the various peoples. To achieve this we need at the same time both the study of the liturgical sources and the day-to-day living experience of the Church enlivened and indwelt by the Holy Spirit.

[24] We have not included in our study the chants either for the post-baptismal eucharistic celebration or for the time of the mystagogy. Suitable chants will have to be provided for the offertory and the communion.

Charles Paliard / *Lyons, France*

The Place of Catechesis in the Catechumenate

Catechesis has not been the most deeply-considered part of catechetical work. In the literature on the catechumenate, it takes on the image of a "poor relation".

There is no reason why anyone should be surprised about that. It is the natural result of a situation in which the essential meaning of "preparing an adult for baptism" was taken as "giving him religious instruction".

We have failed to make clear the prime importance of *conversion* and the principles that govern the communication of the Gospel to adults who ask for the sacraments of Christian initiation. We have also failed to recognize the essential nature and the principles of authentic *sponsorship by godparents,* and to place in their correct interrelation the *liturgical steps* in Christian initiation.

One of the present-day tasks of catechetics is to develop catechesis with the same spirit of invention and loyalty to tradition as has been employed in the other aspects of catechetical work.

I

The Place of Catechesis in Catechetical Work

Catechesis, liturgy and sponsorship by the godparents must be closely *bound up together.* We have here not *three parallel*

88

actions, but just one action, with different and complementary aspects.

1. *Catechesis and Sponsorship*

By means of his sponsors, the catechumen comes into contact with the brotherly communion of Christians and the motherhood of the Church. This is a vital Christian experience upon which catechesis must reflect the light of God's Word. If this experience does not exist, or is too weak, a whole section of the Christian message will remain a dead letter.

2. *Catechesis and Liturgy*

Catechesis and liturgy are closely bound up with each other:
(a) Catechesis discloses *in advance* the meaning of the liturgical acts in which the catechumen is going to participate. It prepares the way for a fruitful participation in the liturgy, because every liturgical act is a profession of faith.

(b) Catechesis makes it possible for the catechumen, *after* the liturgical act, to understand more explicitly everything he has experienced and continues to experience, thanks to this privileged meeting with Christ.

II

What Is the Role of the Catechesis of Initiation?

1. *By This Means, God Speaks to Man*

God reveals himself through his *Word*—God's Word to Abraham, his Word to the people through the priests and the prophets, the Word of God made flesh in Jesus Christ—so that all men can become the children of God.

God never acts without revealing the *meaning* of his action or without permitting man to respond to it with his total being—including his power to know, which is inseparable from his power to act and his power to love.

Catechesis makes it possible for man to meet God as a God

who speaks, for this meeting between man and God should not be purely and simply "unspeakable". Faith is not just a cry.

2. *By This Means, Man Is Able To Speak to God*

"To be born means to be able to speak."

The catechesis of initiation, central to the catechumenate, allows the catechumen to make his own the elementary language of faith (what used to be called the "rudiments" of faith). He can thus participate fruitfully in the life of the community where his faith will constantly be nourished and increased. Without this apprenticeship in the elementary language of faith, he would be like a stranger in the community; he would not be able to take part in its experience, its prayer or its witness. He would not be able to feed on the bread of the Word that the Church provides unceasingly for her faithful.

Catechesis gives God's Word to man in order that man himself may speak. We speak in the Church in *prayer,* which is the word of man to God—but a word permeated by the Holy Spirit; we speak in our *brotherly dialogue,* which expresses our unity in Jesus Christ; we speak in *witness,* through which the Spirit declares to the world, by means of our words, that Jesus Christ is indeed the Savior.

III

THE CONTENTS OF THE CATECHESIS

The catechesis of initiation must transmit "the essentials of the faith". But what are these essentials? Rather than trying to draw up a catalogue of the principal truths that must be believed, it is better to ask: "What will the catechumen need in order to live his Christian life? What acts of faith constitute Christian existence and are characteristic of those who belong to the People of God?"

It is these acts of faith which the *catechesis of initiation must make possible.* Perhaps one might draw out the essential characteristics of the baptized Christian's life of faith as follows:

1. *The baptized Christian is called to proclaim his faith in God and in God's plan by the "I believe in God" of the baptismal service.*

The creed expresses the "articles"—that is, the "articulations" —essential to Christian faith. Each of these has to be a light that reveals the true dimensions of life and the world. It is not enough for the "I believe in God" to be a *formula* known by heart; the faith which the creed expresses has to become the "form" of a life lived.

2. *The baptized Christian is called to nourish his faith and his Christian life in holy scripture.*

Holy scripture is a privileged sign of the never-failing topicality of the Word of God. All the other signs of God's presence do not become God's Word unless they are in one way or another illuminated by scripture. Therefore, the catechumen must have met in scripture the topicality of the Word of the Lord. This does not necessarily mean that he has to become an expert in the Old and New Testaments. The meeting can come about through the medium of just a few texts: the essential is that it must be a real meeting.

3. *The baptized Christian must take part, in faith, in the essential acts of the Christian community.*

The Christian celebrates the eucharist. He is a penitent who is called to receive the forgiveness of Christ in the sacrament of penance. The Christian is called to be a witness of Christ before those who contest, whether explicitly or implicitly, that Jesus Christ alone is Lord. The Christian is called to make his life into a spiritual offering, and thus to participate in the Church's mission of consecrating the world to Christ.

4. *The baptized Christian is called to live out, in the faith, certain fundamental human situations.*

Family life, work, love, suffering and death are fundamental human realities that the Christian, united to Christ, is called to experience as a child of God. As he lives out these realities, he is called to see in them the signs of the presence and of the love of God. All these realities are the occasion for, and, as it were, the material of, acts of faith essential to the Christian life.

It is reasonable to think that by clarifying what is essential to the Christian life in these four spheres I have outlined above, one would be able to "fasten onto" what I am tempted to call the "vital minimum" of the knowledge of faith. In approaching this vital minimum, we can "encompass" the contents of the catechesis of initiation.

IV

THE PROGRAM OF THE CATECHESIS

Throughout the preparation for baptism, in order that the unfolding catechesis may be the servant of a unified faith, one must have a "guiding thread" to follow. What can this be?

The fact that the directors of the catechumenate have up to now proposed hardly any plans or program for catechesis leads me to put forward the following hypothesis: the guiding thread of which we are speaking is not one "simple" thread; it is "composed of"—or should we say "woven out of"—three strands. *The catechist cannot draw up a catechetical "program" to serve a unified faith unless he takes account of three factors.*

1. The Coherence of the Message

The Christian message is coherent and unified. It expresses the unity of God's plan as it unfolds in history. Everything in the Christian message is unified by Jesus Christ and the paschal mystery.

2. The Gradual Entry into the Church

Catechesis, as I have said, illuminates a spiritual experience by making it possible for that experience to turn into knowledge of faith, and to use the language of the faith, and thus to become fully Christian.

Therefore, to know what one is going to speak about at a given moment, one must remember any encounter such as has been described where there has been an authentic experience of sponsorship, or any conversation of that kind between the catechumen and the priest; one must also remember the last (or the next) prayer meeting and the particular liturgical season, as well as the liturgical steps of Christian initiation if the catechumen is approaching one of those steps.

3. *The Catechumen's Human Experience*

The life of every catechumen has its own personal history, distinguished by events to which he reacts by virtue of his environment, his character, his past and his religious nature. Every such event that occurs in his family or professional life, in the world or in the Church—every such personal difficulty or "crisis" can call for a specific catechesis, and may be an occasion for receiving this or that article of the creed with a more personal faith, or for meeting the Lord in some precisely appropriate text of scripture, or for making progress in understanding baptism or the eucharist.

Thus we see the complexity of the "guiding thread" of catechesis and the three "strands" out of which it is woven. The whole art of catechesis consists in weaving them together as tightly as possible so that the catechumen's faith is progressively established as a whole.

V

CONCLUSION

In conclusion, I will simply quote from Vatican Council II's *Decree on the Pastoral Office of Bishops in the Church:*

"Bishops should see to it that catechetical training, which

is intended to make men's faith become living, conscious and active through the light of instruction, should be painstakingly given to children, adolescents, young adults and even grown-ups" (n. 14).

It seems to me that everything I have suggested about the needs of catechesis in the catechumenate is fully in accord with the way in which the Council fathers expressed their teaching mission.

Wilhelm Breuning / *Trier, West Germany*

Baptism and Confirmation:
The Two Sacraments of Initiation

The reformed rite of adult baptism requires a fresh assessment of the appropriate moment for the administration of confirmation. We must consider whether, in this particular use of baptism, it would be beneficial to reproduce the old historical unity between the two sacraments. That the early Church preserved this unity is in itself no sufficient reason why we should do the same. We have to reflect whether, in the case of adults, one should forego a personal meeting with the bishop[1] in spite of the fact that the sacrament's symbolic actions and language would be much more meaningful here than in the case of infant confirmation.

To show that, when combining the two sacraments of initiation, one cannot simply add the rite of confirmation as an independent ceremony to the baptismal rite needs no lengthy proof. But granted that one has some clear idea about the need for a meaningful liturgical relationship between the two sacraments that together constitute initiation, and insofar as one also intends to root this relationship within the liturgical framework, then some degree of clarity about the relationship of baptism to confirmation in the more explicitly doctrinal order is presup-

[1] On the significance of episcopal administration of confirmation, cf. J. Neumann, *Der Spender der Firmung in der Kirche des Abendlandes bis zum Ende des kirklichen Altertums* (Meitlingen, 1963).

95

posed. It is a consideration of the relationship between the two
sacraments in this latter sense that I shall now pursue.

I

THE HISTORICAL ARGUMENT FOR THE COMBINATION
OF THE TWO SACRAMENTS

Acts 19, 5f. testifies that baptism and the imposition of hands
were connected in New Testament times when converts were
received into the Church. Similar testimony is found in Tertullian[2] and other valid sources, making it quite clear that the
practice of administering confirmation immediately after baptism was a basic principle of sacramental initiation procedure
in the early Church;[3] it was regarded as a matter of course and
no attempts were made to consider the two sacraments separately. It is significant that the first unhappy notes come from a
quarter unrelated to the theology of confirmation.

Looking for a simpler method of unequivocally determining
Church membership at a time when heretics were causing considerable trouble, the anonymous tract *De rebaptismatae* de-
valued the imposition of hands—the ceremony that in fact admitted the candidate to the Church community—and thus up-
graded baptism. (Even so, one can also observe in this text the
unquestioning appreciation of the symbolic language of the imposition of hands as indicative of Church community.[4]) Aside
from this disturbance, confirmation and baptism remained so
naturally connected that no special evidence of the link need be
adduced here.

---

[2] *De bapt.*, c. 8 (Corp. Script. Eccl. Lat., 20, pp. 207ff.).

[3] References to individual testimonies of this are readily available in
the handbooks and in other literature on the subject. I shall not allude
to any of them here but shall refer the reader to Burkhard Neuneuser's
summary of the history of dogma on this subject, "Baptism and Confirmation," in Herder's *History of Dogma*, eds. Michael Schmaus and
Aloys Grillmeier (London: Burns & Oates and Freiburg im Br.: 1964).
See also A. Adam, *Firmung und Seelsorge* (Dusseldorf, 1959), pp. 21-
54.

[4] *De rebapt.*, 10 (Hartel: Corp. Script. Eccl. Lat., 3, Appendix 82).

A difficulty arises—and also an obstacle to an understanding of confirmation—when we come to consider the entanglement of this simple two-stage baptism-confirmation structure with a series of other rites which, like baptism and confirmation, have origins rooted firmly in the Church's early years. I refer to the rites of anointing and signing with the cross. The view that considered Christian initiation to mean anointing with the Spirit, just as Jesus thus anointed became the Christ, can be traced back to the New Testament,[5] even though one is not able to infer from these sources a rite of anointing as such.[6] The New Testament also witnesses to an appreciation of initiation as the imparting of an eschatological mark or seal.[7] These images, rich in theological meaning, were earlier dropped from the Church's initiation rites, although not at the same time in every part of the Church. Any attempt to trace the growth of these rites that came to be added to the already existing unity of baptism and the imposition of hands, or to determine when precisely this happened,[8] would, from the dogmatic theologian's viewpoint, contribute little to a solution. Moreover, such is the strength of the unified picture the liturgical historian finds, that there is no point in the process of development at which one's research could fruitfully begin.

However, there is one factor in this tangled story that should not be overlooked, namely, that in some widespread parts of the Church, notably in the East, the ceremony of anointing even managed to supplant the earlier rite of the imposition of hands. The dogmatic theologian can do little more than note with some alarm that in the earliest Eastern theology of confirmation (Cyril of Jerusalem) the initiatory imposition of hands and,

[5] 2 Cor. 1, 21f.; 1 Jn. 2, 20. 27.

[6] Rudolf Schnackenburg, *Johannesbriefe* (Freiburg im Br., [2]1963), pp. 152f.

[7] 1 Cor. 1, 22; Eph. 1, 13.

[8] Cf. H. Elfers, "Gehört die Salbung mit Chrisma im ältesten abendländischen Initiationsritus zur Taufe oder zur Firmung?" in *Theol. u. Glaube*, 34 (1942), pp. 334-41, where Elfers takes up B. Welte's analysis in the latter's *Die postbaptismale Salbung, ihr symbolischer Gehalt und ihre sakramentale Zugehörigkeit nach den Zeugnissen der Alten Kirche*. Freib. theol. Studien, 51 (Freiburg im Br., 1939).

particularly, the biblical texts that witness to it play no part at all.[9] It should also be mentioned that the Scholastic theology of confirmation showed similar attitudes on this point. But whatever the variety of procedure, what is important is that wherever one looks, one finds a relatively clear witness to what was evidently regarded as the basic two-stage structure of initiation. This fundamental underlying factor remains intact, however one divides up the larger number of individual rites.

II

THE INCREASE OF BAPTISMAL GRACE

Agreement that full initiation into the Christian life should invariably take this two-staged form appears—at least at first sight—to be the only unbroken thread in theological tradition on this subject. In the early Church East and West were agreed that both stages, at least in all normal situations,[10] should take place consecutively. The subsequent intrusion in the West of a temporal and still prevalent separation of the two stages is clearly shown to be a secondary and historical development. The not unjustified adherence to the episcopal administration of confirmation—although this procedure had not gone entirely unopposed[11]—ultimately led to the temporal separation of the two stages. But to show that this development is a secondary one historically is not to judge its value. As regards the normal case —that is, infant baptism—one would in fact be inclined to give preference to Western practice, without necessarily condemning Eastern practice. The following thoughts on the subject should show clear reasons for this preference. (The question, however, takes on a very different shape as regards adult baptism.)

---

[9] *Cat. myst.*, 3: *P.G.*, 33, pp. 1087-94.

[10] Separation did occasionally occur—e.g., in the case of emergency baptism. Cf. the Synod of Elvira, *Denzinger-Schönmetzer (DS)*, 120.

[11] Cf. *DS*, 215 (Innocent I). The explicit summons in Acts 8, 14-17 appears to precede a period of unconsidered practice that automatically regarded the bishop as the one who should administer the sacraments of reception into the Church.

It must first be noted that the difference in practice regarding confirmation connected with or separated from baptism—where the two-stage nature of the introduction to the Christian life was generally recognized—before it ever gave rise to theological speculation, must have aroused various notions that had their effect on the theological explanation of what is at stake. Wherever the two rites were administered in the one ceremony their relationship could be effectively described only in terms of the complementary polarity between the two processes.

Their separation gave rise to an explanation in terms of a growth analogy: confirmation is the sacrament of fully-developed Christian maturity. The Scholastic theology of confirmation adopted this view completely, seeing in confirmation an *augmentum gratiae baptismalis*. Such an interpretation suffers from the difficulty of explaining the meaning and significance of an eventful, once-and-for-all growth of this type, for growth is a continuous development through the living power of a beginning. Admittedly maturity is a new stage. But to locate the achievement of this maturity in another event is to falsify the original analogy—namely, growth through the living power of a beginning. Then, also, such a growth has to be made possible through appropriate nourishment. But if baptism and the eucharist are well suited in this respect, it becomes still less clear where confirmation fits in.[12] It is hardly surprising, therefore, that in sorting out the effects of confirmation we are left with only a very vague notion of *augmentum gratiae*.[13]

Traditional piety compensates for this lack of clear substance by connecting confirmation to the "special gifts" of the Holy Spirit. This is a heritage from ancient liturgical practice and from the patristic theological attitude to confirmation. But the subsequent separation of baptism and confirmation dulled still further the Western Christian's already limited feeling for the

[12] One must of course be quite clear about the limitations of the growth analogy. We are concerned not with a biological growth but with growth through personal encounter in which Christ is nourishment in the personal sense.

[13] Cf., for instance, the total poverty of Trent's statements on confirmation: DS, 1628-30.

Holy Spirit. It need not in itself be harmful to regard the grace of confirmation as *donum speciale Spiritus Sancti* (special gift of the Holy Spirit). The extraordinary magisterium's clearest pronouncement on confirmation[14] tends in this direction. Vatican Council II picks up the same theme again,[15] although significantly giving it ecclesiological depth. But even Vatican Council II makes no clearer how confirmation brings about the "more perfect connection with the Church". It is precisely this point that theology must seek to substantiate: Why is the baptized person through an ecclesial-sacramental act once again given a *donum speciale* of the Holy Spirit?

As already suggested, there grew from this correct understanding of confirmation as the *donum speciale* of the Holy Spirit more than just a promotion of the pneumatic understanding of the Christian life. The first step is to show that our understanding of the *donum speciale* rests on our recognition of the Holy Spirit as *donum*, and this in full and proper accordance with his trinitarian and salvation-historical role as such. To suggest that he is himself *donum* for any other reason is to diminish his role. In other words the pastorally proper separation of infant baptism and confirmation led—incidentally through the deeper Western premises of trinitarian theology[16]—to a diminution of the function of the Holy Spirit in the initiation process. Baptism simply was not considered—although precisely because of its separation from confirmation it was most important that it should have been—with reference to the particular role of the Holy Spirit as the gift of salvation *tout cours*.

[14] *DS,* 1319: "The Holy Spirit is given as a strengthener, just as he was given to the apostles at Pentecost, so that the Christian can confess the name of Christ with courage."

[15] *Constitution on the Church* (n. 11): "The bond that ties them to the Church is made more complete by the sacrament of confirmation. It enriches them with the special strength of the Holy Spirit and gives them a stricter obligation to act as true witnesses of Christ, by spreading and defending the faith through word and deed."

[16] Trinitarian theology's assessment of the unity of the divine nature, as found in the successors of St. Augustine, corresponds with the tendency in the doctrine of grace to take a stronger interest in the created effect whose efficient cause can only be the whole Trinity.

Thus, although it was possible in connection with confirmation to talk of *donum speciale,* it was precisely the "specialness" of it that remained shrouded in mystery because no one had seen or worked out the implication of the fact that the Holy Spirit is himself the gift of salvation. Consequently it was impossible to contrast the *donum speciale* in its particular sense with the gift of justification given through baptism.

III

RETURN TO THE PATRISTIC THEOLOGY OF CONFIRMATION

Faced with this sort of dilemma, it is hardly surprising that people are now trying to get around the extremely tricky notion of confirmation as an *augmentum gratiae baptismalis* by returning to older sources.[17] One can hardly talk of growth where baptism and confirmation are received within a few minutes of one another. Undoubtedly, what actually happened forced the development of a corresponding explanation: the connection between baptism and confirmation had to be seen as a much closer one. And as has been seen, the combination of the two rites in one ceremony is a practice as old as the New Testament itself. The two sacraments together constitute initiation. But how do they do this? That confirmation complements baptism we have already seen. It is necessary to emphasize at this point that since the early Church did not think in terms of a sequence of seven sacraments, she showed no burning desire to consider separately the two stages that served to make up initiation—at least not in

[17] An account of the positions adopted by French theologians is provided by P. de Vooght in "Discussions recentes sur la confirmation," in *Paroisse et Liturgie,* 6 (1954), pp. 409-13. See also the Anglican theological controversy between Gregory Dix, *The Theology of Confirmation in Relation to Baptism* (Westminster, [3]1953) and L. Thornton, *Confirmation: Its Place in the Baptismal Mystery* (Westminster, 1954) on the one side; and, on the other, G. Lampe, *The Seal of the Spirit* (London, 1951). M. Thurian, in his *La confirmation: consecration des laïcs* (Neuchâtel and Paris, 1957), shows evidence of having been influenced by Dix. Thurian's book has a very comprehensive bibliography.

any conceptually specific manner. Nevertheless, there was a recognized distinction between the two stages and it is of interest to us now to note what this was.

Blurred though the borderlines might be, one meets several variations on the theme that confirmation is the "completion" of baptism.[18] These variations are not necessarily mutually exclusive, and they are found to be stated with varying degrees of precision. In the contemporary appreciation of confirmation the influence of these patristic concepts is to be found in notions of the following type:

1. Baptism primarily effects the remission of sin, whereas confirmation more positively imparts the Spirit's life-giving grace.

2. Confirmation is the final "sealing" of the baptized person because it bestows the fullness of the Spirit.

3. Baptism links the individual's fate to the crucified and risen Christ whereas confirmation confers upon him a share in Christ's messianic priesthood.

4. Baptism is to confirmation as the paschal mystery is to the mystery of Pentecost.

But a close look at these theories shows that, although they are fine thoughts, they solve none of our problems, particularly if one is concerned to do a little more than split hairs.

The first point obliges one to ask: If baptism presents and effects a life relationship with the crucified *and* risen Lord, how does the two-stage nature of the rite in fact amount to two sacraments, remembering that what is at stake is one indivisible reality? [19]

It must first be said of the second point that the sacramental "conveyance" of man to Christ effected through Christian initiation is already regarded in the New Testament as the eschatological sealing of Christ through the Spirit.[20] This being so, the

---

[18] Cf. A. Adam, *op. cit. supra*, footnote 3, pp. 39f.

[19] Cf., for example, *Apost. Konstitut.*, 7, 22, 2 (Funk, II, p. 406). See also Neunheuser, *Baptism and Confirmation*. In addition cf. Karl Rahner's approach to a modern definition of confirmation in *The Church and the Sacraments* (London: Burns & Oates and Freiburg im Br.: Herder, 1963), pp. 90-93.

[20] Cf. 2 Cor. 1, 22; Eph. 1, 13f.

differentiation that would call this process "confirmation", the second stage in the initiatory sequence, represents a secondary development.[21] In what way, for example, does the Christian who has received baptism and confirmation at different times thereby become eschatologically "more completely" sealed or marked than through his baptism alone? Is the sealing process a separate stage in itself?

It seems sufficiently evident that in this secondary development the notion of "sealing or marking" has undergone an alteration: confirmation seals that which takes place in baptism. In fact, confirmation would now appear to be the seal of baptism. But why is this form of sealing needed? The answer to this question should be evident from the nature of the process itself.

Bishop Cyril of Jerusalem's christological and pneumatological view of confirmation, which through its positive union of christology and pneumatology is at the root of the third point,[22] seems to be the most profound confirmation theology of the patristic period. However convincing might be the imagery presented by the comparison between the Christ who emerged from the waters of the Jordan and *then* received the Spirit, and the anointing of Christians *after* baptism, one still has to ask if it is not so that the real nature of Christian baptism lies in the truth of the statement that it is precisely over the waters that the Spirit stirs. Or are we to believe that the one mystery of Christ is divided into a paschal mystery and a messianic mystery of the Spirit?

Having asked that, one has asked the appropriate question of the fourth thesis for the purpose of determining the relationship of the paschal mystery to the pentecostal mystery in terms of the difference between the (first) risen and (then) Spirit-sending *Kyrios*. And with this same question in mind, one's impression is

[21] Cf. A. Adam, *op. cit.*, pp. 48-50, and F. Dölger's important analysis, *Sphragis. Eine altchristliche Taufbezeichnung in ihren Beziehungen zur profanen und religiösen Kultur des Altertums*. Studien zur Geschichte und Kultur des Altertums, V (Paderborn, 1911), pp. 3-4.

[22] *Cat. myst.*, 3, 1-2: *P.G.*, 33, pp. 1088f. Similar ideas are to be found today in Schillebeeckx's work: *Christ, Sacrament of the Encounter with God* (New York: Sheed & Ward, 1964).

confirmed that the astounding fact about the patristic witness on this subject is the extent to which it regarded the two-stage structure of the initiation rite as self-evident and clear beyond need of any special explanation. But the theology of the Fathers offers small help when one's concern is to justify the two-stage structure of the rite in terms of the nature of salvation offered to mankind through the Church.

IV

THE PASCHAL MYSTERY AND THE PENTECOSTAL MYSTERY

It seems to me that when we ask ourselves about the relationship of baptism and confirmation we are in fact involved in an examination of the relationship of Easter to Pentecost. Both New Testament exegesis and liturgical studies leave one with the firm impression that the relationship is all but theologically evident. Even when the intrusion of the extraordinarily crude notion that Pentecost is the feast of the Holy Spirit has been surmounted in favor of a more christological and salvation-historical theology, we still tend to separate the two by declaring that Easter is the glorification of Christ while Pentecost is the sending of the Holy Spirit through the glorified *Kyrios*. However, this view is at variance with an older celebration of Pentecost that, notwithstanding the witness of Acts 1—2, remained innocent of any attempt at such a separation.[23] It not only embraced death and resurrection as a unity—a conception to which we have now reverted—but also included in this unity the sending of the Holy Spirit. This approach is in accordance with the New Testament proclamation as most specifically expressed by John.[24] The sending of the Spirit is not, in the form of a new salvation event, an addition to the Easter mystery, but is the profoundest salvation impulse of the glorification of Jesus.

Therefore, in Acts, in apparent opposition to this unified

[23] Cf. R. Cabie's analysis in *La Pentecôte: L'évolution de la Cinquantaine paschale au cours des cinq premières siècles* (Tournai, 1965).
[24] Cf. Jn. 7, 39.

view, do we simply have a different theology that would separate
by fifty days the outpouring of the Holy Spirit from the Easter
event? Or do we also have here a case of a far less facile division
of the one mystery of Christ, a presentation of two aspects of
salvation history—also, be it noted, to be found in John[25]—in
which Easter and the sending of the Spirit are conceived as a
unity?

The most notable point about Easter from the historical angle
is that although all is completed through Easter, the story does
not end there.[26] On the one hand, the Church exists in the
mystery of the paschal completion, in the "once and for all" [27]
of the Jesus returned to his Father. On the other hand, it is
precisely within this state that her freedom lies, within which
the one mystery of Christ can take form. Stated differently, this
is to say that precisely for the paschal and once-and-for-all completion to be shared by all mankind, Easter cannot itself be the
end of the road; one must move on from that center. But this
necessary ongoing process is not primarily the history of a collection of individuals, but rather the history of the Church, the
history of a family, growing from its first brethren. It is with
this shaping of the Church that Acts is concerned. We see the
Church taking on form not beyond Easter—as regards the
quality of the completion there are no expectations *beyond*
Easter—but from Easter. But this history of which we speak is
not a piece of theatrical skirmishing after the event but is the
Church struggling to find her true structure, and in this struggle
it is not the Church who establishes her structure but the Holy
Spirit who, through his gifts (charisms) builds up the Church
as *he* wishes. And we know that this Spirit will never forsake
the apostolic Church by withdrawing his assistance.

Predictably another question arises at this point: How does
the Church include mankind in this polarity of her own paschal
Christ-reality—a polarity that, on the one hand, consists in the

[25] Cf. the texts on the Holy Spirit.
[26] Cf. Lk. 24, 44-49.
[27] Heb. 9, 12.

Church's corporate unity with the consummated Christ now returned to the Father (who from the outset did everything for
his Church), and, on the other hand, consists in the fact that
here on earth is the appointed place in which the salvation community, in genuine human terms, is able repeatedly to re-create
itself?

V

ACTS 8, 14-17: THE IMPOSITION OF HANDS IN SAMARIA

Once again it appears that Acts can come to our aid, although
its answer is not explicit. Naturally I suffer from no delusion that
the motive behind the report of Acts 8, 14-17 is to set out the
doctrine of confirmation. Nevertheless, this account is still *the*
significant one from the point of view of confirmation, and the
more so because of the larger context in which it is set. Becoming
a Christian and being admitted to the service of the charism-
dispensing Spirit are processes that Acts regards as closely linked
with one another.[28] As the account shows, in Samaria it is precisely these charisms, the bestowal of which is so closely linked
to the admittance of a new member to the ecclesial community,
that remain wanting as long as the missionary Church so newly
established there—and in which Christ has already been proclaimed and baptism administered—is not in personal touch
with the Church of the apostles. It is only this personal contact
with the Church of the apostles, brought about by Peter and
John laying their hands upon the members, that releases the
community's charismatic potential. Of course it cannot be maintained that the charisms are connected with the laying on of
hands in any concrete way. The Spirit breathes where he wills.[29]
The point is that it is in the Church of the apostles that he

[28] Cf., in this context, 19, 6 and 10, 44. Amazing here is the fact that
the Spirit comes even before baptism.

[29] Not without reason does the 8, 14-17 pericope stand in the larger
context of the Simon Magus story. The story makes it quite clear that
it is not the apostles who control the Spirit but vice versa.

breathes. This is the field in which the paschal salvation mystery of Christ takes shape. That Church's growth is the result of the Spirit's charisms operating in the different situations prevalent in the different stages of history. This Spirit is himself the gift of salvation, but he also finds a role in his service for each individual within the Church as this ever becomes more like Christ.[30]

We have now outlined an ecclesiologically-based answer to the question of the two-staged nature of admittance into the Church: the Church includes a man in her once-and-for-all time-completed paschal mystery, which is both christological and pneumatological, through the baptism of Christ. As the body to whom the mystery of Christ is entrusted, the Church receives him as one destined to contribute to her concrete historical shape, and she enables him to perform his structural role by including him through confirmation in a personal way in the concrete apostolically-structured community.

Seen in this light the traditional view of the grace of confirmation takes on validity: confirmation confers the Spirit through whom one is able to witness to Christ. What is important is that this way of thinking about confirmation is freed from the isolated reasoning the traditional view has given it by basing the arming of the individual with the charismatic gifts on propositions that, being too personalistic, are insufficiently ecclesiological; this view also does not overlook the precondition that mediates the particular charismatic spirit: the mediation of the Holy Spirit as the gift of salvation in its paschal fullness that occurred earlier at baptism. In other words, the relationship to the Spirit that confirmation brings about presupposes the earlier establishment of the fundamental baptismal relationship with the same Spirit.

Looking at confirmation in this way, it should not be too

---

[30] Catholic exegesis' ancient and deep-rooted unwillingness to explain this passage as referring to the "charismatic Spirit" no longer exists. Cf. J. Gewiess, *Die urapostolische Heilsverkündigung nach der Apostelgeschichte*. Breslauer Studien zur historischen Theologie, N.F.V. (Breslau, 1939), p. 128; A. Wikenhauser, *Die Apostelgeschichte*. Regensburger NT, V (Regensburg, ³1956); H. Schlier, *Die Zeit ker Kirche* (Freiburg im Br., 1956), p. 116.

difficult to suggest the time liturgically most suitable for its administration. Because of its own special role as an event that involves the candidate in such a very personal and demanding way, its separation from baptism is more appropriate in the case of infant baptism. Notwithstanding this separation, confirmation still remains in a very real sense a part of the initiation process.

However, when adults are being received, it would be much more meaningful to combine both aspects of initiation, inasmuch as the willing surrender to Christ (baptism) requires its complement (confirmation), which is the affirmation of the call to cooperate as a member of the concrete Church. The conjoining of the two stages is in this case the natural prerequisite for the initiation-completing reception into the eucharistic community. For the sake of consolidating the power of meaning present in the initiation process when thus understood, it would be preferable to resituate the force of its message in the more appropriate setting. This wealth of meaning is certainly to be found in the episcopal administration of confirmation, particularly in the case of adult baptism.

PART II
BIBLIOGRAPHICAL
SURVEY

Luciano Borello, S.D.B. / *Turin, Italy*

Liturgical Reform and Sacred Music in Italy

Introduction

In Italy the liturgical reform did not take pastoral efforts in the field of sacred music completely by surprise; the "Cecilian" movement had prepared the way by means of an intelligent and unified effort that had already yielded considerable fruit. Nevertheless, we must admit that the proclamation of the most recent documents on the matter[1] has given a completely new orientation both to musical production and to pastoral efforts.

Consequently, any attempt to provide a brief analysis of the present state of affairs must of necessity distinguish the various stages through which the problem has evolved. These stages can be outlined as follows: (a) before the 1958 Instruction; (b) from the 1958 Instruction to Vatican Council II's *Constitution on the Sacred Liturgy;* (c) the present situation.

In the interests of greater clarity and brevity we will limit our observations solely to that sacred music directly related to the Mass.

Before the 1958 Instruction

Until 1958 the repertoire of popular sacred music comprised only:

---

[1] We refer especially to the Instruction of September 3, 1958, Instruction *On Sacred Music and the Liturgy,* the *Constitution on the Sacred Liturgy* of Vatican Council II and the Instruction *Inter oecumenici.*

(1) Latin chants for the Ordinary of the Mass, plus a few hymns, several sequences and the responses to the dialogue with the celebrant and ministers;[2]

(2) Italian chants for the recited Mass.[3]

With respect to the first category, we can point out that only relatively few parish communities achieved a reasonably adequate repertoire and execution, despite the commendable zeal exhibited by pastors of souls.

Chants in the second category were faced with the inconvenience of remaining completely apart from the true and proper liturgical action, limiting themselves to serve the celebration as "explanatory chants" at the various parts of the Mass: Introit (*Gloria*), Offertory (*Sanctus, Agnus Dei*), Communion and Dismissal.

This may account for the inadequate development of such chants.[4]

From the 1958 Instruction to Vatican Council II's Constitution on the Sacred Liturgy

Upon the appearance of the Instruction on Sacred Music and the Liturgy (1958), pastoral effort was confronted with new perspectives: the creation of a repertoire of chants that could be inserted in great part into the liturgical action. This gave rise

[2] In this sphere the situation was very varied and disparate. However, we can restrict ourself to what comprised the common patrimony: the Mass "De angelis" and the "Missa de requiem". Two popular Masses were also used very widely (though to a lesser extent): "Missa Cantate domino" of Oltrasi and "Missa laus tibi Christe" of Caudana. Also part of the common patrimony were various Gregorian hymns and a few of the better known Latin chants (such as *Lauda Sion, Pange lingua, Adoro te devote, Ave verum,* etc.).

[3] Among the most popular we might cite: G. Haydn, *Messa popolare* (Florence: Maurri); L. Refice, *La Messa dei fanciulli* (Rome: AISC); D. Bartolucci, *I canti del popolo per la Messa* (Rome: AISC); M. Scapin, *Canti per la Messa* (Milan: Eco); M. Pagella, *Canti per la Messa* (Turin: L.D.C.); N. Vitone, *Cinque canti per la Messa* (Turin: L.D.C.).

[4] One collection of chants for the recited Mass deserves particular mention: *Il popolo alla Messa* (Milan: Regalità). It is perhaps the most serious attempt to provide a set of chants that are directly functional for liturgical celebration. However, it has not achieved wide distribution.

to a rich output of chants for the recited Mass which soon became the patrimony of a good deal of the Italian parishes.[5]

Up to the present time, they are still the most widespread chants, primarily on account of two factors:

(1) the new character of the musical form—it is a question of chants in responsorial form;

(2) the determining influence of records which facilitate learning such chants—all those mentioned have been recorded.

Although these chants have had the merit of "breaking the ice" in many traditionally intractable assemblies, they have also quickly revealed their limitations, for the following reasons:

(1) They are, in the main, musically inferior.

(2) The responsorial form (having become exclusive) has resulted in unduly leveling (and thus impoverishing) the chant of assemblies.

(3) The shortsighted enthusiasm for "the new chants" has drawn attention away from the Latin patrimony which, for many assemblies, constituted a valid instrument of active participation.

(4) The insufficient preparation of pastors of souls and the lack of vision on the part of those responsible have prevented an adequate selection from being made among the excessively rich repertoire prepared in most cases with empirical tastes or with predominantly commercial preoccupations.

This partially explains the strong reaction on the part of musicians and many "right-thinking people" to an output that is wrongly identified with "the new music demanded by the liturgical reform". Moreover, attempts to adjust the situation, as of the present time, have not yielded satisfactory results.[6]

[5] We list the most notable: Gazzera-Damilano, *Canti liturgici per la Messa letta* (Rome: AISC); Gazzera-Damilano, *Fanciulli a Messa* (Milan: Eco); Bosio-Lasagna-Loss-Stefani, *Canti per la Messa dialogata* (Turin: L.D.C.); A. V., *I canti dell'Assemblea* (Bologna: UTOA); Moneta-Molfino, *Plebs sancta* (Milan: Eco); N. Vitone, *Cinque canti per la Messa* (Messina: LES); A. V., *La Messa del fanciullo* (Turin: L.D.C.).

[6] We allude above all to the constitution of the Association ECAS (Editori canti a scheda) which advocates a preventive examination of the chants—whether from a musical or from a textual and liturgical point of view.

Separate consideration must be given to various attempts at chanting psalms in Italian,[7] even though they can under many aspects be considered in the same vein as the other chants because of the indiscriminate usage to which they have been put both within and outside the liturgy.

Despite widespread use of the psalms, they seem to pose more of a problem today than ever before. It is a problem that cannot be resolved by means of a puerile imitation of form (or thoroughgoing polemic), but solely by means of a serious study concerning the value and function of the psalm in the liturgy.

The Present Situation

Vatican Council II's *Constitution on the Sacred Liturgy* and the beginning of the reform sanctioned by the "Inter oecumenici" have signaled a new turn with consequences that are readily foreseeable but difficult to evaluate. Indeed:

(1) The reform does not concern only the chant of the faithful but the chant of the entire assembly: celebrant, ministers, choir and people.

(2) The introduction of the vernacular into the liturgy has unexpectedly posed the problem of the chant of the "proper"—until then considered the exclusive property of the choir.

(3) However, the most delicate problem (because it is completely new for musicians) is the one concerning the diverse structures and musical forms required by liturgical celebrations.[8]

These represent too many problems of an excessively complex nature to be seriously faced by persons who are indeed zealous but often unprepared or in some way prevented from working

---

[7] We regard the most serious to be *Trenta Salmi ed un cantico* (Turin: L.D.C.). This is a translation from the original Hebrew, utilizing the Gelineau modes together with antiphons of Italian composers. The complete edition of the *Salterio corale* also contains the "simple modes" of Dusan Stefani, adapted for alternative choral recitation.

There is no dearth of other attempts, among which we might mention that of Fr. Colombo, *Salmi per l'anno liturgico* (Brescia: Quiriniana)—but in general it is simply a question of (more or less conscious) imitations along the path opened up by Gelineau.

[8] In this respect, cf. what has been written in the specialized periodicals *Eglise qui chante* (France), *Musik und Altar* (Germany), *Il canto dell'Assemblea* (Italy), in monograph-issues edited in common.

under better conditions. The situation was rendered even more difficult since pastoral effort demanded that something be done, for the liturgical reform had begun! This explains why scarcely a year after the liturgical reform of the Mass (March 7, 1965) the Italian output of sacred music destined for Mass appeared to be enormous from the quantitative point of view.

An analysis of this music might be made as follows:

(1) The most numerous output concerns the Ordinary of the Mass, which as of the present time has received more than fifteen musical settings—whether intended for the people,[9] reserved to the choir[10] or destined for both choir and people.[11] However, we must admit that, with few and praiseworthy exceptions, the settings in question are of an inferior quality, exhibiting little liturgical sensitivity and modest technical mastery.

(2) The music for the "proper" has taken two separate paths: (a) the integral liturgical text given in the Missal has been set to music;[12] (b) the antiphon has been reduced to a brief refrain and psalm verses added.[13] While taking account of the serious character of the work, we greatly doubt the quality of its results. Apart from the fact that the present official text was not drawn up with music in mind, we are still confronted with the basic problem of the function of the individual chants of the proper.

(3) As regards the music for the celebrant and sacred ministers (tones for the readings, orations, preface, Our Father and the dialogues with the assembly), there was no time to reflect. On October 7, 1965, the Episcopal Commission on the Liturgy gave interim approval to the tones and melodies that had already been approved for the diocese of Lugano (Switzerland). These

[9] The majority of these have been published in *schede Ecas,* 6/52-115.

[10] The most promising attempts seem to be those of P. Santucci, *Missa vulgaris* (first, second, third, fourth) (Bologna: Migrizia).

[11] We refer to the *Messa Vaticano II* of L. Picchi—monodic in origin but arranged for two, three and four voices alternating with the people (Bergamo: Carrara).

[12] Significant examples have appeared in the periodicals *Musica Sacra* (Milan) and *Ecclesia Cantat* (Bergamo).

[13] The periodical *Armonie di voci* (Turin: L.D.C.) has published a relevant issue, based on the *Messale dell'Assemblea,* which has adopted the same principle.

have not received enthusiastic acceptance (perhaps because of the speed with which they were issued), but only experience will be able to judge their worth.[14]

(4) In the meantime, the output of generic chants for dialogue Mass has diminished.[15]

(5) We attach significance to the interest in the chorale and the strophic hymn which has recently borne appreciable fruit. Three different working areas can be distinguished: (a) transcription of ancient (especially German) chorales with substantial fidelity to music and text;[16] (b) adaptation of ancient chorales to a text arranged in free style as regards content and form;[17] (c) creation of original strophic hymns as regards both text and musical structure, inspired by Latin texts.[18]

The first solution seems to be the weakest, while the second and third appear to offer good working prospects for the creation of a valid repertoire as regards both music and text. Above all, chorale and strophic hymns, which take their inspiration from the various liturgical seasons, have decisive pastoral importance.

Conclusion

We are, therefore, in the presence of an impressive resurgence of activity that the pioneers of the "Cecilian" movement in Italy may possibly have dreamed of but never actually realized. Are we then to conclude with a positive judgment? Only in part! Unfortunately, quality does not always correspond to quantity. The polemics between the opposing factions demonstrate not only that there is a lack of agreement about concrete evaluations (which is inevitable) but also that there is no common basis of understanding for the purposes of a dialogue.

[14] *Toni per il celebrante* (Bergamo: Carrara). Reprinted in the *Messale quotidiano latino-italiano* (Turin-Leumann: L.D.C.).

[15] The most recent examples have come from the music firms Eco (*Schede Ecas* 6/121-124) and Carrara (*Ecas* 6/102-110).

[16] A certain number have appeared in the *schede Ecas* published by the music firm Eco (Milan), but the most important case is the edition of *80 corali di Bach* transcribed by P. Santucci (Bologna: Nigrizia).

[17] See the adaptations of G. Stefani which appeared in the *schede Ecas* 10/24-28.

[18] The best of this type are those of the *Centro di Liturgico di Lugano*, some of which appeared in the *schede Ecas*.

The composer works instinctively, impelled by unavoidable pastoral demands; the critic operates from positions that are considered fitting but often not demonstrated.

There is a need for precise ideas—whether from the liturgical or from the musical and pastoral points of view; there is need for dialogue and the exchange of experience; above all, there is a need for directives—even to guide the experiences that are being attempted.

Therefore, we welcome the appearance of the periodical *Il canto dell'Assemblea* as a highly positive step.[19] Its very purpose is to favor common study and to direct experiences toward a clearly understood end. It can be a first step; the rest will follow as a consequence.

[19] The periodical is edited by the *Centro Catechistico Salesiano di Torino-Leumann* in conjunction with the periodicals *Eglise qui chante* (France), *Adem* (Belgium), *Musik und Altar* (Germany), *Katholische Kirchenmusik* (Switzerland) and *Church Music* (England).

Domingo Cols / *Barcelona, Spain*

Sacred Music in the Perspective of Liturgical Renewal

The recent history of sacred music in Spain, considered in relation to the scheme of liturgical renewal put forward by Vatican Council II, can be divided into three main stages.

I

THE SITUATION UP TO 1955

The *Motu proprio* "Tra le sollicitudini" of Pope Pius X in 1903 initiated two currents of reform: (1) the liturgical movement, centering the whole of the Church's worship around the liturgical celebration of the mysteries of the life of Christ, and linking up later with pastoral renewal; (2) the reform of sacred music along the lines laid down by the pope. Unfortunately, these two currents ran along parallel lines, and it was a long time before they met.

Church musicians explored three main avenues of development during this period. There was the "Gregorian Movement" dedicated to promulgating the beauty and sanctity of Gregorian chant as a vehicle for the Church's liturgical prayer. Its success, at a time when sacred music was in a state of decadence, was rapid and so extensive that several Gregorian melodies became

117

popular songs. Its effectiveness, however, was progressively limited by the fact that its protagonists failed to pay sufficient attention to pastoral needs, because of a false conception, in some quarters, of the meaning of liturgical worship, and because of the failure to appreciate the actual capacities of a liturgical assembly. This led to the formation of elite groups of Gregorian enthusiasts practicing their art outside the context of liturgical assemblies.

Another movement, led by several great musicians, sought to give tone and splendor to liturgical celebration through the musical techniques—in themselves excellent—of polyphony and the organist's art. Its achievements were likewise limited in the end, due to its failure to fulfill two fundamental requirements which pastorally-based liturgical theory was later to make clear: (1) "full understanding and active participation" by all the faithful in the liturgy; (2) the *munus ministeriale,* the help that each musical piece used in the liturgy must bring to the understanding of the whole liturgical structure.

The third movement was an attempt, through popular musical idioms, to help the people to realize the festive character of their prayer and their faith. This attempt usually took the form of providing musical background for popular acts of devotion or an extension of a "private" form of liturgical celebration, as a result of the strict conditions laid down for the musical components of the public liturgy. The main trouble with such songs was the inadequacy of their texts to the forms of prayer that increased pastoral understanding showed to be desirable.

But whatever its failings, this era produced a great deal of work and paved the way for fruitful later developments. It produced many musicians whose compositions did the Church a great service: J. Valdés, N. Almandoz, N. Otaño, G. M. Suñol, P. Donostia, P. Iruarrízaga, L. Romeu, L. Millet, L. Urteaga, P. Prieto, P. Altissent and P. T. de Manzárraga, among others.

II

FROM 1955 TO THE CONSTITUTION ON THE SACRED LITURGY OF 1963

This phase cannot in fact be separated from a preparatory period that began in 1945 when the application of pastoral principles to the liturgy began to affect vital sectors of the Church. A realistic approach to pastoral problems, biblical studies and the renewal of catechetics forced pastors to realize the unsuitability of many elements in the Church's musical heritage. The crisis of sacred music was at its height in 1955 when Pius XII issued his encyclical *Musicae sacrae disciplina,* which allowed the use of popular sacred music in the liturgy and unleashed a spate of musical compositions in this idiom, some of them somewhat extreme in expression. This was inevitable, and a long, calm effort was needed to guide this proliferation along suitable lines. Various Centers of Liturgical Pastoral Work and other institutions took charge of this work of renewal, following the requirements of the pastoral clergy.

The St. Pius X Institute at Salamanca has done a great deal of intelligent work, directed by J. Rodríguez Medina. In Tomás Aragüés it has found a composer of excellent popular melodies, some of which are new and highly original approaches to the musical problems of liturgy today—his processional chants, for example.

The Barcelona Center of Liturgical Pastoral Work, whose activities embrace every aspect of the subject, has also worked on the different aspects of post-conciliar sacred music, and its influence has spread beyond Catalonia to the whole of Spain. Its musical team, led by A. Taulé, J. Ubeda and the present writer, has collaborated with many outside composers to change the musical atmosphere of the liturgical assembly.

Montserrat, through the work of Dom I. M. Segarra and Dom G. Estrada, has produced psalms, hymns and canticles, popular in character and perfectly in accord with the musical tradition of Catalonia, which again have spread to enrich liturgical assemblies throughout the whole of Spain. The Montserrat psalmody (Segarra) follows the basic Gelineau pattern, but with a different tonal character. The first series published has been adapted for use in France. Together with the Barcelona Center and others such as "Hogar del Libro", Montserrat shows the liturgical and musical vitality of a region which has been wonderfully rich in outstanding musical talent during this century.

Two other teams have adapted French sacred music to Spanish requirements: "Hechos y Dichos", under the personal direction of Gelineau himself, has provided an adaptation of his psalms, about which I shall say more later, and "Berit" has adapted many of the rich melodies of Fr. Deiss.

The publication of a general catalogue, indexing the collections from all the various Centers, has opened the way to a more general collaboration among musicians throughout the country.

III

THE FUTURE

The promulgation of the *Constitution on the Sacred Liturgy* has enabled definitive steps to be taken in liturgical music, such as settings for the Ordinary of the Mass and some of the chants of the Proper. The acceptance and continued viability of these naturally depend on various other factors and cannot be forecast with any accuracy at present. What is certain is that there are several major problems requiring common effort on the part of the pastoral clergy, liturgists and musicians if the liturgical renewal is to mature and take root in the very heart of the assembly of the faithful. These are:

1. The adaptation of the mentality and efforts of ecclesiastical musicians to the spirit of the Council. This is a nationwide task.

2. Revision of the methods of musical training in the institutions that specialize in this in the Church.

3. A determined effort to bring the people into the sung liturgical celebration. This is particularly important and realiza-

ble in Spain where the people's heritage of popular and folk songs is so rich. A deep study of the structure of popular Spanish music would reveal unsuspected technical aspects.

4. The musical recitation of the psalter in itself and as an essential element in the chants of the Mass. New experiments will still have to be made here, since the Gelineau psalmody has not proved easy to adapt to the rhythmic patterns of the Spanish language. The Episcopal Commission is about to publish a standard translation of the psalter, which will lead to new attempts to find a suitable musical framework for it.

The sources to which musicians have looked for inspiration for their new melodies suggest this reflection: the musician, although he need not always be saying something new, must always be saying something interesting, making use of musical elements that spring from mastery of new technical developments and that have already reached those sectors most alive to artistic renewal.

Stephen Somerville / *Toronto, Canada*

Sacred Music in Canada
and the United States

Catholic church music was a rather tedious subject in North America until a few years ago. The first sign of new life could be said to have appeared in 1958, following the famous Instruction of the Sacred Congregation of Rites on music. But still more life has flowed into the musical body since Vatican Council II and the great *Constitution on the Sacred Liturgy*.

The subject is now vast and interesting, and sometimes fascinating. I cannot begin to do justice to it in one short article, so these remarks are necessarily sketchy and based on my own fragmentary experiences in certain areas of English-speaking Canada (especially Toronto) and the United States.

The condition of church music today shows great promise and vitality and excitement. Nevertheless, there are great areas of imperfection. The well-known fossilization of Catholic liturgy until recent times had applied to music as well, with a consequent separation from secular music. There was an understandable lack of scholarly and episcopal leadership, as well as a mentality which wanted musical matters to be laid down once and for all in black and white regulations. There was no single musical culture uniting the people, for they were mostly recent immigrants of various ethnic sources. What native music did develop seemed very remote from worship, except, of course, the Negro spirituals.

The great change came in the winter of 1964-1965. It seems to me that it came too suddenly. While a few creative parishes and other centers had been quietly developing new and healthy forms of church music, the majority were told that on a certain Sunday they could (and probably "must", or else "must not one day sooner") sing the Mass in English and sing congregational hymns at low Mass.

This may have been good shock therapy; at least it caused a flurry of comment in conversations and newspapers. But it neglected the law of gradual growth and made many pastors and musicians feel a helplessness and anxiety because it was simply impossible to do everything at once. The malaise is disappearing. Over the years it was comforting to visit places like Grailville, the main center (Loveland, Ohio) of the Grail Movement, where genuine church music was growing.

The restoration of hymn-singing by the congregation is now a feature of North American Catholic churches. Sometimes it seems to testify to obedience rather than enthusiasm, and sometimes the repertory is monotonous. But newly published hymnals are competing eagerly to improve matters. *The People's Mass Book* (World Library of Sacred Music), *Our Parish Prays and Sings* (The Liturgical Press, St. John's Abbey), *The Hymnal of Christian Unity* (Gregorian Institute of America), *The Book of Catholic Worship* (The Liturgical Conference), *The English Liturgy Hymnal* (F.E.L. Publications)—these are well-known titles, and there are numerous others. There is a general desire for updated hymnals.

Some of these books run to 800 pages, due to a large mass of supplementary texts and ritual. I question such size, especially at a time when further drastic changes are just around the corner and when we need to stress the value of liturgical looking and listening.

Until recently, one rarely heard a "Protestant" hymn in a Catholic church. Now it is common to find a growing list of the best old hymns from our brethren of other denominations. Sometimes the words have been modernized or replaced. There is an encouraging number of hymn-writers producing new texts.

It is probably true that pruning is needed to control the growth of new hymns. This is certainly true of new Masses. The Ordinary of the Mass has appeared in published musical settings innumerable times. Three hundred is a rough guess. As chairman of the Toronto Music Commission, I began with a brave effort to appraise them all as they appeared. I soon gave up. At any rate, the verdict of time is perhaps more important. I found a frequent lack of liturgical balance. For example, many a Creed was written for a four-part choir or in a complex melodic line. Many a *Kyrie* tried to be an overture.

Dr. C. Alexander Peloquin has given considerable prestige to the English sung Mass by his exciting works. His *Mass for Choir, Congregation, Organ and Brass* has been performed on some major occasions with real éclat. He has done many other sacred compositions.

The Propers of the Mass are receiving increased attention. The Summit Series (World Library of Sacred Music) by contemporary writers is a serious effort to produce liturgical art. A general weakness in the Proper chants is a rather rigid fidelity to the texts of the Roman missal. At low Mass in many parishes it is the practice for everyone to recite (not sing) every word of these fragmentary texts, with no distinction between verse (cantor) and antiphon or responsory (congregation or choir). Even the editors of the pocket and leaflet missals that are used seem blind to the sung and alternated nature of these parts of the Mass, and, of course, to their ultimate inadequacy as modern processional chants. At the time of this writing, we are awaiting the publication of the *Graduale Simplex,* which should improve the situation of the Proper chants. In February of 1966 the National Council on Liturgy (Music) of Canada made a considerable improvement by recommending the substitution of a suitable popular chant for the *Introit,* etc. They did not, of course, attempt to authorize the omission of the missal text, but rather noted that it "need not be read aloud".

We all know the old distinction between "high" and "low" Mass. Fortunately, in Canada and the U.S.A., this distinction is fading, and congregations feel free to sing as much or as little of the Mass as circumstances suggest.

What about Gregorian chant? It, too, is definitely waning. But at first there was a widespread effort to convert it to English. It was somewhat dismaying to see publishers with competing versions. Imagine half a dozen *different* English settings of Mass XVI or the Requiem Mass! And some places are probably singing them yet. But more creative talents have since come forward. Meanwhile, the experts assure us that Gregorian chant should only be sung with its Latin text. Does this mean it will not be sung at all, or scarcely? Will the values and the beauties of the old chant at least inspire modern composers?

Nearly everyone is interested in the psalms. The first and greatest catalyst was the work of Fr. Gelineau translated into English. The standard North American psalter is the "Confraternity" version, and this is proving fairly resistant to singing. But psalms are being composed here and there. Predictably, some workers are trying to save the Gregorian psalm tones. The International Committee for English in the Liturgy is hoping to produce a definitive good English psalter for liturgical and musical use. This will be a great boon and encourage composers by furnishing an international market.

Canadian and U.S. priests are now singing the Prefaces in English. Their translations are different, but the music is similar, being the traditional ferial tone. I know that Archabbot Rembert Weakland, O.S.B. and others are concerned to try new tones as well.

"Folk Masses", with their folk-type chants and guitar accompaniment are now an international phenomenon, but they seem to be truly flourishing in North America. At times they have caused violent controversy, and repressive measures have prompted organized picketing or lively public discussion. Here I must be brief. The student congregations at these celebrations seem to create and find a genuine experience of community and eucharist that might well be denied them elsewhere. Even adults attend regularly. For some the type of music may be a passing attraction. But there is no reason why folk music for worship should not and cannot have quality of its own, even if the fare is not very solid. The main lesson of the folk Masses to the "rest of us" is probably not so much musical as liturgical and communitarian. They are a healthy reaction against the stuffiness of many a parish Mass.

I have attended such Masses at St. Michael's College in the University of Toronto,[1] and they were most worthwhile. Many recordings have appeared. The most famous is probably that of Fr. Clarence Rivers, a Negro priest in Cincinnati. His Mass, which reflected the Negro spirituals, definitely helped to launch the folk Mass movements.

A common lament among certain musicians is the dissolution of Church choirs and the disappearance of the old masterworks of sacred music. I find the complaint a bit puzzling. It is true that Gregorian chant and Latin selections in general are going out. It may also be true that many good choirs are disbanding, though I have scant evidence of this. The main fact seems that Gregorian chant and polyphonic Latin music were usually sung either badly or in a museum-like setting, or both. The one is a musical evil, the other a liturgical one. Thus, far from deploring the present situation, one should rejoice that a new broom has swept clean, that the vine-dresser has pruned and plucked the branch so that it may bear fresh fruit.

There is an immense field for fruitful musical growth in the North American Church. But it is still evident that good musicians are in short supply, and also that they need to meet the

[1] One of the significant institutions for Sacred Music in Canada is St. Michael's Cathedral Choir School. It was founded in Toronto in 1937 by the late Msgr. J. E. Ronan, P.A. The school has 240 day students from Grade 3 to Grade 13—that is, to the end of high school and university entrance. In addition to a complete academic curriculum, it provides a full basic training in music. All the boys (aged 8 to 18) take choral training and sing in one of five choirs; they also study piano, gradually moving on to music theory, harmony, organ, counterpoint and all the basic requirements of the Royal Conservatory of Toronto. Many of the graduates have become organists and choirmasters in parish churches. The school is affiliated with the Pontifical Institute of Sacred Music in Rome.

liturgists. In other words, much education is needed. The task of education is being faced, and there is a strong organization for it in the Liturgical Conference, which has its headquarters in Washington and stages a liturgical week annually in a large city, with generous emphasis on music. There are many other colleges and institutions that teach music. There are means for liaison with countries like Holland, France and Germany, where very positive results have already been achieved and stand available.

Once again, I underline the sketchy nature of this account and my limited experience of a manifold subject. It remains for other North American observers to review the scene again.

Moira Kearney / *Durban, South Africa*

Sacred Music in South Africa

Before attempting to assess the progress we have made and the general level at which church music finds itself at present, it may be well to bear in mind the problems presented by the vastness of our country, its division into so many different language groups and its comparatively small Catholic population. This population comprises roughly 835,000 Africans, speaking six or seven different Bantu languages; 300,000 White and Colored, speaking English and Afrikaans; and small numbers of Indians and Chinese—in all, just over a million.

Since their conversion to the faith, the Africans have been singing in their own languages in the style characteristic of most mission countries until quite recently. This usually meant that while the priest said Mass silently at one end of the church, the congregation provided an accompaniment of prayers and hymns occasionally related to what was going on at the altar. The hymn tunes in vogue in South Africa were mainly of German and French origin, and the Bantu words were adapted to their meter and rhythm regardless of the requirements of language and style.

Now that the true participation of congregations is being promoted and vernaculars have been accepted as liturgical languages, efforts are being made to provide suitable church music

128

for various Bantu languages. A successful conference was recently held at the Lumku Missiological Institute in the diocese of Queenstown, where an enthusiastic and representative gathering of teachers, composers and priests was guided by two leading authorities on African music. Several new Masses by African composers were submitted, some portions of which were acclaimed as worthy contributions and a significant forward step in the evolution of Bantu church music.

One of the great handicaps to progress is the difficulty of finding people who still retain an intuitive appreciation of the Bantu idiom while possessing a musical culture adequate for composition. South Africa has suffered more than any other part of Africa from the Westernization of its indigenous population. An important point that emerged from the Lumku Conference was the need for Africans to benefit from advanced European techniques, while still maintaining their own idiom. To fill this need there came a proposal to assist African composers by providing study weeks from time to time under the supervision of competent university professors. This will be of great assistance to the regional language commissions which, in association with the National Language Commission, are endeavoring to develop Bantu liturgical music.

As regards the English-speaking congregations, the problem that confronted us when the vernacular was introduced was an obvious one—the almost complete non-existence of Catholic church music in English. Fortunately, quite a number of suitable compositions are now available from other countries. Experience has taught, however, that we cannot recommend these compositions indiscriminately, but must make a careful selection. Many of the products of this transitional period have been written in a pseudo-Gregorian idiom totally unsuitable for modern languages.

With regard to English and Afrikaans, the two centers mainly engaged in the promotion of liturgical music are Stellenbosch, in the archdiocese of Cape Town, and Durban. The Dominican Fathers of St. Nicholas Priory in Stellenbosch have produced a

Mass Book in English and Afrikaans with suitable hymns and the text of the processional chants for Sundays and feast days.

Durban's first effort was the publication of a collection of hymns suitable for use during Mass. In true ecumenical spirit it borrowed heavily from the musical treasures of other Christian bodies. More recently a Catholic Library of Sacred Music has been established as a publishing and distributing center. Overseas music is selected and recommended and local compositions are published. The emphasis in local compositions is on responsorial singing. A sincere attempt is made to give due importance to the texts and to reflect the spirit and meaning of the words.

For the purpose of encouraging more active participation among our congregations, our church choirs meet periodically. Their experiences are related and their efforts combined, resulting in great enthusiasm for further research and progress. These gatherings have proved most stimulating, and we feel sure the benefit has been felt in most of our parishes, where congregations are noticeably more aware of their part in the liturgy. When leadership is given by the clergy, the people gradually lose their reserve; they will, before long, be contributing in no small way toward real unity in worship.

South Africa was represented at the International Conference for Church Music and Liturgy, held in Fribourg, Switzerland, in 1965. The experience proved an invaluable one, giving us insight into the development of European countries who have already many years of progress and experiment behind them. News of this conference has aroused considerable interest, and a genuine effort is being made in our churches to provide music of the highest quality and of a suitable character worthy of the new liturgical demands.

The National Liturgical Commission of South Africa has its subcommittee for sacred music, and it is hoped that a national conference will soon be held, to which leaders in liturgical music will be invited from Europe to share their experience with us and to give us information of the very latest developments in church music.

The outlook of our school children is realized as a very vital contribution, and an earnest attempt is being made to educate them in the spirit of the liturgical renewal, thereby ensuring that they will not be hindered by the inhibitions of so many of our elder generation. The schools are having regular instruction in church music by trained musicians, and we feel we have no better assurance of the success of our future singing congregations.

This sums up the situation as it exists in our part of the world. We are a comparatively young country which naturally lacks the centuries of tradition which European and other nations have, but it is with patience and hopeful expectation that we look forward to the future. Fortunately we are blessed with able leaders, both liturgical and musical, and we have every confidence that our humble efforts can hold their own with other countries of similar resources.

Amaro Cavalcanti de Albuquerque / *Rio de Janeiro, Brazil*

Sacred Music in the Liturgical Renewal in Brazil

The movement for liturgical renewal in Brazil now includes a vigorous attempt to fit sacred music into a dynamic ministry, in accordance with the principles laid down by the Council. Although some of the former obstacles remain, there are signs of a genuine renewal throughout the country's vast, almost continental expanse. In spite of the paucity of composers of sacred music and our complete lack of institutes specializing in sacred music, a real musical movement is unfolding with the support of the excellent Joint Pastoral Plan of the National Conference of the Bishops of Brazil.

In April, 1962, that Conference's Emergency Plan had already anticipated the awakening of the ministry, pointing out the urgent need for the formation of communities devoted to faith, worship and charity. Isolated efforts began to show results, especially in the musical enterprises attempted. Since 1960 a version of some psalms, set to Gelineau's music and published by the Rio de Janeiro Archdiocesan Committee, has attained an incredible circulation. The courses on pastoral music, originally run under the Committee's guidance, were repeated in several of the country's larger cities, thus helping the distribution of the first song sheets for use by congregations. New horizons were opened and these first attempts were helped forward with the introduction of the vernacular to the liturgy and the consequent renewal required by the Council.

In 1965 the approval of the episcopate's Joint Pastoral Plan found fertile ground for the recommended programs of action. Recent compositions had already introduced the congregation's singing as an essential component of the intended participation. Courses in pastoral singing had been very well received by the religious communities; nowadays, sung participation is the norm in schools, colleges, seminaries, etc. Under the demands of pastoral renewal, these communities had a decisive influence on parishes. Especially in the large cities, parishes now count on the help of seminarians who are greatly aiding the increase in singing by the faithful.

Songs for congregations are being disseminated at a surprising rate, not only in the large cities but also in the most remote corners of missionary areas. Certain songs, for instance, have achieved the same sales in three years as the most popular French songs in eight years. Having been first published without either great aspirations or special resources, these editions of song sheets for use by congregations have proved remarkably successful: in contrast with European countries, our communities are now renewing themselves with the help of these minor contributions, uniformly and without internal conflict. It is obvious that there are still no songs of profound value, nor can it be said that the existing ones are entirely satisfactory. But in what is a still developing nation, sacred music is not encountering obstacles to the development of a truly liturgical-musical ministry. Composers of sacred music are gradually achieving recognition. They are participating in a great effort of adaptation, and even in joint planning. Meanwhile, even extra-liturgical religious music is receiving definite and continuous attention.

A task of considerable responsibility was given to the National Committee of Sacred Music created in 1965 by the Bishops' Conference: to accelerate the musical movement, which was already under way, and to study the bases for profound and efficient pastoral action. As a first step, it held (July, 1965) the First National Conference on Sacred Music (in Valinhos, São Paulo) at which the musicians engaged in the movement for the renewal of liturgical music were present. The main theme was the study of bases for the possible use of the essentials of our own Brazilian music, since this displays such fabulous riches. Ninety percent of our popular sacred songs are "imported" and, although accepted by the people, have neither made their mark with the modern Brazilians, especially the young, nor satisfied the basic requirements of the movement of renewal. At the Conference Father José Geraldo de Souza, S.D.B., presented to the musicians a paper on "The Problem of Brazilian Musical Expression in the Liturgy".

On the other hand, in an attempt to place the subject in a pastoral context, Father José Alves de Souza, music master of the Rio de Janeiro Seminary, produced a work entitled "Musical Program for a Liturgical Ministry" which examined the forms of composition suitable to an active and full sung participation by the congregation.

In 1966 the Second National Conference was held in Recife, where a step forward was taken with the joint study under the general theme "Practical Possibilities for the Adaptation of Brazilian Music to the Liturgy". To this debate were invited lay musicians who, together with liturgical musicians, started examining the characteristics of melody, harmony and rhythm of musical form and instruments that might be suitable for use in the liturgy. Thought was also given to methodology and to actual musical techniques to be used in the work.

These first steps taken by the National Committee of Sacred Music will certainly lead to further development of our sacred music. This first advance is backed up by others of no less importance for the future. In 1966 the Higher Institute of Liturgical Ministry was founded under the direction of the Liturgical Secretariat of the Bishops' Conference. At first this will have a Department of Sacred Music, an embryo for a future Institute. With the cooperation of prominent musicians in the regional Committees on Sacred Music, the number of new compositions has increased. Already several Masses have been composed in a pastoral style. The National Committee, in collaboration with the publisher, Editora Vozes de Petropolis, has begun publishing a series of basic works intended to form an easily accessible body of reference. The whole of our vast country has been reached by this publisher's work, of which an example was the publication of various composers' musical texts for Holy Week accompanied by a good quality record.

In summing up, we consider that Brazil has already begun, as seen from the above-mentioned indications, a movement of musical renewal. Imperfections and faults are inherent in the early stages of any enterprise. But the promise of greater and profounder attainments fills our musicians with hope. This is especially true when we see that the Brazilian people are so given to music in all its forms. Singing is essential to the Brazilian. On account of this, at Vatican Council II the Holy Father, by especially reminding the Brazilian bishops that "a people who sing are a people who pray", exhorted them to develop pastoral action in Brazil through poetry and music which, he felt, were sensitive chords of the Brazilian's psychology.

Reinhard Kösters / *Sudhagen, West Germany*

Conditional Baptism

In certain circumstances, Catholic Canon Law makes provision for the administration of baptism in a conditional form—either a conditional first baptism, or a conditional rebaptism. Such a *baptismus conditionatus*[1] becomes necessary when there are serious doubts whether a particular person is in a condition to receive valid baptism. For in this case (as the law is normally interpreted today, at any rate) baptism might prove to be null, which would be derogatory to the dignity of the sacrament. On the other hand, to refuse baptism altogether would be to act contrary to the necessity of this sacrament for salvation. Thus, the institution of conditional baptism in Canon Law is entirely in accordance with the general principles of Catholic law concerning the sacraments, which requires that the sacraments instituted by Christ in the new covenant are to be administered and received "with the greatest care and reverence".[2]

When it comes to detailed interpretation, ecclesiastical law expressly examines any doubts—in the case of a miscarriage—whether the infant to be baptized can be considered truly human, whether it is still alive at the moment of baptism, whether it can, if need be, receive baptism on some other part of the body instead of the head and, for someone who has reached

[1] Codex Iuris Canonici (CIC), Can. 763, §1.
[2] Cf. *ibid.*, Can. 731, §1.

the age of discretion, whether he freely desires baptism.[3] Finally, the law of the Church envisages the possibility of a doubt—especially in the case of foundling children[4]—whether a person has been baptized at all, or whether the baptism was valid.[5] In all these doubtful cases, there is some question whether the person is capable of receiving the sacrament of baptism validly; therefore, in each case Church law provides for "conditional baptism".[6]

In any case, conditional baptism will only achieve its purpose of safeguarding the dignity of the sacrament if it is worthily administered. This is more especially true of conditional rebaptism: in no circumstances must careless administration of conditional rebaptism obscure the once-for-all character of baptism. Baptism must, therefore, only be repeated in its conditional form when there is a reasonable doubt (*dubium prudens*) about the fact or the validity of a previous baptism.[7] In the concrete case of foundlings, it is expressly laid down that an attempt must first of all be made to remove the doubt in question by "careful inquiry".[8] In accordance with this proviso, Fr. Sola,[9] for example, insists that a mere suspicion with regard to the fact or validity of a previous baptism does not justify a conditional repetition of the sacrament. But he adds that in the case of baptism, the requisite doubt—in view of the necessity of this

[3] Cf. *ibid.*, Cans. 748; 747; 746, §3; 752, §3.

[4] Cf. *ibid.*, Can. 749.

[5] Cf. *ibid.*, Can. 732, §2.

[6] The use of the subjunctive "conferantur" in Canon, 732, §2 implies an imperative note in the baptismal regulations which is absent from those for confirmation and ordination; cf. K. Morsdorf, *Kirchenrecht*, II (Paderborn, [1]1961), p. 22.

[7] Cf. Can. 732, §2.

[8] Cf. *ibid.*, Can. 749. An instruction of the Holy Office issued in the year 1860 requires that there also be a careful previous examination of any doubts about the intention of the person receiving baptism: (DS 2838). Canon 733, §1 refers to the *Rituale Romanum*, where there is added to the conditional baptismal formula the necessary instructions under Canon Law: "Hac tamen conditionali forma non passim aut leviter uti licet sed prudenter et ubi re diligenter pervestigata probabilis subest dubitatio. . . ."; II, 1, 9. In similar terms, cf. the *Catechismus Romanus:* p. 2, De Sacr. Bapt., n. 57.

[9] F. Sola, *De Sacramentis Initiationis Christianae, Sacrae Theologiae Summa* IV (Madrid, [4]1962), p. 170, n. 101.

sacrament for salvation—does not need to be as serious as in the case of confirmation; a reasonable doubt will suffice.[10]

The cases where conditional baptism is held to be possible and requisite from the legal point of view are extraordinarily rare, especially as the formerly more frequent cases of its use for foundlings seldom come into the picture now. On the other hand, the only case where conditional baptism may even be of the greatest contemporary importance is not expressly mentioned in the *Codex Iuris Canonici*: namely, the use of conditional baptism for Christians who come into the full fellowship of the Catholic Church from a non-Catholic Church or Communion.

The rule still applicable to this case is set out in a decree of the Holy Office dated Nov. 20, 1878.[11] True, this decree does not require that every convert should as a matter of course be conditionally rebaptized; such a practice would be quite obviously contrary to the definitive recognition at the Council of Trent of baptism performed (in due and proper form) even by heretics.[12] The requirement is rather that there should be an examination of each individual case. However, baptism should be conditionally repeated not only when there is still a reasonable doubt (*probabile dubium*), but also when the inquiry into the particular case does not bring out anything specific either for or against the validity of the first baptism.

In so providing, the decree does not indeed adopt the rigorous attitude of a synodal statute of Paderborn, issued in 1867, in which it was laid down that in view of the actual position, it should be assumed that baptism outside the Catholic Church was invalid.[13] This decree may be taken to justify a general doubt of baptism administered outside the Catholic Church and to sanction conditional rebaptism in individual cases, although it does

[10] Cf. *ibid.*

[11] DS 3128.

[12] Sess. VII, *Decr. de sacramentis*, Canones de sacramento baptismi, can. 4: "Si quis dixerit, baptismum, qui etiam datur ab haereticis in nomine Patris et Filii et Spiritus Sancti, cum intentione faciendi quod facit Ecclesia, non esse verum baptismum": DS 1617.

[13] Archif. f. Kath. Kirchenrecht 20 (1868), p. 357.

not assume either the validity or the invalidity of such baptism, but rather its doubtful validity. It must indeed be admitted that the duty of examination in individual cases, which this decree makes more stringent, has up to the present been only very superficially observed, and has often in fact been widely disregarded. K. Morsdorf states that "the usual practice until now" has been "to administer conditional rebaptism in all cases of reconciliation to the Catholic Church".[14]

On the evangelical side, it is considered a scandal from the ecumenical point of view that the decree of 1878 should contain this presumption of a general doubt about the validity of baptism administered outside the Catholic Church, and even more so that there should be this rather widespread practice of ignoring the duty of examination in individual cases and rebaptizing all converts conditionally as a matter of course. In a recent statement put out by the United Evangelical and Lutheran Church of Germany (VELKD) there is the following expression of opinion: "The Evangelical Church must, on the other hand, beware lest the Roman Catholic Church should show scant respect to her baptismal rite, although the order of all the Evangelical Churches requires that it should be administered in the name of the Trinity, and with water. The Roman Catholic practice is all the more objectionable in that it is a common Christian principle, recognized since time immemorial even in the Roman Catholic Church, that baptisms duly performed according to the proper rites are to be considered valid." [15] The theoretical and, even more, the practical questioning of the validity of baptisms administered outside the Roman Catholic Church is all the more calculated to arouse bitterness in Evangelical circles at the present time when Vatican Council II specifically stressed the ecumenical significance of baptism.[16]

[14] K. Morsdorf, art. Tanfe (VI. Kirchenrechtlich) *Lex Theol. u. Kirche* IX, 1320-1322; 1321.

[15] Amsbl. d. VELKD I, n. 9, of Nov. 10, 1957.

[16] Cf. *Constitution on the Church* (n. 14); also cf. *Decree on Ecumenism* (nn. 3, 22).

Meanwhile, however, the ecumenical dialogue on the theory and practice of conditional baptism is under way, encouraged greatly by H. Asmussen's "Fünf Fragen an die Katholische Kirche".[17] Asmussen is particularly concerned with the irregular *practice* of conditional baptism for converts to the Catholic Church. This is to be distinguished from the question that is also at issue between the confessions: namely, the justification *on principle* of conditional baptism. This is the question we shall now proceed to consider.

A few years ago F. Lau gave fundamental consideration to "Conditional or Tentative Baptism and the Justification for It in the Lutheran Church".[18] Lau's study was prompted by the emergence of a possibility among the committees of the VELKD dealing with the various sects that baptism as practiced by particular groups (e.g., the *Christengemeinschaft*) would not be recognized as Christian baptism. This has brought up the question whether conditional baptism might not provide a way around the difficulty of making a decision on this particular point that would be generally binding.

In examining this matter, Lau is therefore concerned with inquiring whether conditional baptism is basically possible from the point of view of Reformed theology and its interpretation of scripture.[19] Lau comes to a negative conclusion, and in so doing he supports his systematic considerations by historical evidence regarding the treatment of cases of doubtful baptism by the undivided Church in the early Middle Ages. This historical evidence does indeed throw some light upon the earlier history of conditional baptism between the years 800 and 1200, but Lau maintains that this has left few traces; he was only able, in fact, to discover two in the 9th century.

[17] H. Asmussen, "Fünf Fragen an die Katholische Kirche," in *Una Sancta* II (1956), pp. 127f. The questions are repeated—with due note taken of the answers received—in *Die Katholizität der Kirche,* ed. H. Asmussen and W. Stahlin (Stuttgart, 1957), pp. 375f.

[18] F. Lau, "Die Konditional—oder Eventualtaufe und die Frage nach ihrem Recht in der Luteramische Kirche," in *Luther-Jahrbuch* 25 (1958), pp. 110-140.

[19] *Ibid.,* pp. 112f.

Lau particularly stresses the fact that conditional baptism is unknown in Gratian's Decree, contrary to the misleading quotations sometimes found in Catholic works. Although, according to Lau, W. Jetter is not quite correct in his remark with reference to Gratian that "conditional baptism had not yet been invented",[20] yet it may (in Lau's view) "be quite definitely accepted that up to 1200 the Medieval Church as a whole knew nothing of conditional baptism"; however, following these traditions of the Fathers and the decrees of the early Church, she looked upon a baptism that had probably been carried out, but was not certainly attested, as lacking in objectivity; in such cases she reserved judgment about it and rebaptized unconditionally.[21] It was not until Pope Alexander III's time, he maintains, in connection with and more particularly under the authority of Thomas Aquinas, that conditional baptism became established in the Church and, incidentally, that the doctrine of the indelible character of a sacrament played a leading part.[22]

Lau then goes on to deal in detail with Luther's adverse attitude and his desire to see conditional baptism as such banished from the Church, because he held that it settled nothing, denied nothing, affirmed nothing, conceded nothing and removed nothing.[23] Luther, he says, was primarily concerned that the Church should have an assured witness to baptism, and that she herself should be able to give assured testimony of a baptism. A baptism that the Church knew nothing about was for Luther no baptism at all.[24]

According to Lau's interpretation, Luther's decision should be reaffirmed since it is rooted in the deepest possible evangelical

[20] W. Jetter, *Die Taufe beim jungen Luther* (Tübingen, 1954), p. 36, n. 2.

[21] F. Lau, *op. cit.,* pp. 119ff.

[22] *Ibid.,* pp. 121f.

[23] In a letter of May 12, 1531, Luther wrote to W. Linck: ". . . baptismum conditionalem simpliciter esse tollendum. . . . Et ratio nostra haec est quod conditionalis nihil ponit neque negat neque affirmat neque dat neque tollit. . . ." This is referred to and discussed by F. Lau, *op. cit.,* pp. 126ff.

[24] *Ibid.*

concept of the objective nature of baptism, which alone guarantees that "the forgiveness of my sins is publicly assured to me in my baptism by God and before the community in an irrefragable fashion". On the other hand, "conditional baptism has always existed in the Church, but only as an expression of the indelible character implanted by baptism, *ex opere operato*, acting, as it were, automatically and quite independently of faith".[25] From this point of view, Lau maintains, objection should also be raised to the line taken by J. Höfling,[26] the only theologian of importance in the Evangelical camp to give express support to the idea of returning to Catholic baptismal practice,[27] apart from the Anglican Church which has always practiced conditional baptism up to the present day.[28]

From the Catholic side, A. Hollerbach has joined issue with Lau.[29] He calls attention to references to conditional baptism at a very much earlier date—at the end of the 4th and at the beginning of the 6th centuries—and he makes it clear by a number of further facts and arguments that conditional baptism may in general be called "an institution of the early Church" and that its roots certainly lie closer to the authoritative origins of church order that has until now been supposed.[30] Hollerbach especially calls attention to the fact that testimony in the early Church right up to the time of Gratian in no way regards a doubtful first baptism as "lacking in substance".[31] In his systematic discussion of the problems raised, he protests against too closely linking the (High Scholastic) doctrine of the sacramental character of baptism with the subject of conditional baptism, for there is historical evidence refuting this in the practice of the Eastern Church. In spite of her rejection of the doctrine of

[25] *Ibid.*, p. 136.
[26] J. Höfling, *Das Sakrament der Taufe nebst den anderen damit zusammenhängenden Akten der Initiation* (1846).
[27] Cf. F. Lau, *op. cit.*, p. 124, n. 46.
[28] Cf. *ibid.*, pp. 138f.
[29] A. Hollerbach, "Zur Problematik der bedingten Taufe Existenz und Ordnung," in *Festschrift für E. Wolf* (Frankfort, 1962), pp. 122-54.
[30] *Ibid.*, pp. 126-30.
[31] *Ibid.*, pp. 130, 142.

the indelible character of baptism, she has always practiced conditional baptism, and continues to do so to this day.[32]

Moreover, Hollerbach ascribes to Lau an insufficient understanding of the Catholic doctrine of indelibility. He refers to a definition by K. Rahner[33] and asserts that a properly understood doctrine of the sacramental character of baptism is hardly in any way at variance with the Reformed Churches' teaching about the objective nature of baptism.[34] And, finally, great importance should be ascribed to Hollerbach's contention that the condition attached to the baptismal formula is not a "genuine" condition, but only has the force of a declaratory statement and is not in itself absolutely necessary. It comes very close, in fact, to the "baptismal exhortation", also recommended by the committee of the VELKD in parallel conditions.[35]

At this point it may be useful to summarize the discussion about the proper use of conditional baptism for converts. The historical material bearing on the theology and practice of this matter since the Council of Trent has been brought together in a monograph by R. Stehfen written some time ago, but not yet superseded.[36]

In answer to H. Asmussen, F. Thijssen[37] objects that in the Evangelical doctrine on baptism there is a lack of the requisite "intention". Because the Evangelical Churches do not call attention to the purpose to do at least what the Church does, Catholics naturally presume the existence of "a real danger that baptism is not being administered as the Church baptizes", and

[32] Ibid., pp. 140f., 127.

[33] K. Rahner, Kirche und Sakramente (Quaestiones Disputatae, 10) (Freiburg, 1960), p. 79; the sacramental character consists "from the point of view of its content in the adoption into the Church of the person baptized by means of a sacramental act taking place at a definite moment".

[34] A. Hollerbach, op. cit., p. 141.

[35] Ibid., p. 140.

[36] R. Stehfen, Die Wiedertaufe in Theorie und Praxis der römisch-katholischen Kirche seit dem tridentinischen Konzil (Marburg, 1908).

[37] F. Thijssen, "Sakrament und Amt bei den nicht-katholischen Christen. Versuch einer autwort auf die fünf Fragen von D. Hans Asmussen," in Una Sancta 14 (1959), pp. 82-108, esp. pp. 87-94.

it is not easy, in Thijssen's view, to remove this presumption. In his opinion, therefore, it would probably not be wrong to suggest that there are good grounds for the requirement of examination in each separate case, and a general assumption that there should be rebaptism *sub conditione*.[38]

But Thijssen's doubts about the Evangelical intention are not shared by A. Hollerbach.[39] He quite rightly supports his opinion by referring to an essay by S. Tromp.[40] Since particular defects in the *form* and in the *matter* (such as baptism by sprinkling, which is generally rejected today) do not justify any general doubts about the validity, Hollerbach maintains that baptism as administered in the Evangelical Churches today should be presumed to be valid. "Unless there is a clear demonstration to the contrary, it should be assumed that a baptism performed in the name of the Trinity, and with water, within the fellowship of a Church knit together by ecumenical bonds, is *per se* valid." [41] In this opinion, Hollerbach is clearly and deliberately going beyond the rule laid down by the Holy Office in the decree of 1878.[42]

A similar conclusion is reached at the same time and quite independently by F. Haarsma.[43] This verdict carries all the more weight in that it represents the considered opinions of E. Schillebeeckx, F. Thijssen and F. Haarsma, under the leadership of J. Wetermann, as a result of joint discussions on the subject of the validity of baptism.[44] Haarsma is particularly critical of "a certain . . . over-scrupulous tutiorism latent in the sacramental teaching".[45] The present existing form of a baptismal certificate,

[38] *Ibid.*, p. 94.
[39] Cf. A. Hollerbach, *op. cit.*, pp. 147f.
[40] S. Tromp, "SC Concilie die 19 Junii 1570 de baptisme Calvinistarum seu de intentione ministri," in *Divinitatis* 3 (1959), pp. 16-42.
[41] A. Hollerbach, *op. cit.*, p. 151; cf. pp. 146f.
[42] Cf. *ibid.*, p. 150.
[43] F. Haarsma, "Die Gültigkeit der Taufe in nicht-katholischen Kirchen," in *Una Sancta* 17 (1962), pp. 181-87 (originally: "De geldigheid van de doop in niet-katholieke kerken," in *Tijdschrift Theol.* 2 [1961], pp. 171-77).
[44] *Ibid.*, p. 181, n. 1; cf. p. 172, n. 3.
[45] *Ibid.*, p. 186; cf. p. 187.

subscribed to by one of the most important Protestant communities in Holland, which he mentions by name, is in his view a sufficient safeguard. For the communities included in the German Evangelical Church it would seem that the same holds true, to judge by a recent utterance of E. Stakemeier on the subject of conditional baptism.[46] "It can be said in general that not only are the baptismal regulations identical in purpose, but also that the various Church authorities are concerned to see they are duly and properly carried out, both by the instruction of candidates for baptism, and by inquiry when official visitations take place." [47] It would seem to be an urgent ecumenical task to consult directly with all the Evangelical Churches and communities concerned so as to make it possible to achieve recognition of their respective baptismal rites and then confine the duty of examination in individual cases (with converts, for example) to examination of the baptismal certificate of the Church in question.

[46] E. Stakemeier, "Zum ökumenischen Gesprach über die bedingte Taufe: Kath. Nachrichten—Ag.," in *Konzil-Kirche-Welt* 8/9 (1966), pp. 8-12.

[47] *Ibid.,* p. 10.

PART III

DO-C DOCUMENTATION
CONCILIUM

Office of the Executive Secretary
Nijmegen, Netherlands

Evangelization and
the Catechumenate in the
Church throughout the World

INTRODUCTION

A rapid glance at the following contributions is enough to show that they do not pretend even approximately to be geographically complete. We have information on a few countries only. It is reasonable that Holland and Germany are not included since the contributors from these countries have written other articles for this present volume and have consequently given an impression of the situation in their countries. The absence of the United States and Poland, for example—where, as in France, the situation has changed as far as evangelization and the catechumenate are concerned—would be indefensible if we were not taking soundings but endeavoring to give a total geographical picture of all the countries in which the Church is present.

These soundings, however, are not arbitrary. Of the seven countries treated here, three belong to the old maternal soil of Christendom: France, Spain and South America, the latter having the same type of Christianity as Spain and Portugal. Three have relatively young Churches: Africa, Formosa and Vietnam. In the former group Christianity is closely interwoven with the culture of the countries; in the second group evangelization has found itself faced with an existing culture with which it has had to try to live in harmony. One might regard Japan as a bridge between the old Christianity and the new contemporary Japan which has also borrowed from the West elements other than those of Christianity. Nevertheless, the agreement in the evangelization and catechumenate as found in these three very different cultures is striking.

Thus, the necessity of the renewal of the catechumenate appears everywhere, whatever the method that is envisaged for its realization, as well as a personal confrontation of the candidates for baptism with the whole contents of the Gospel. One might say, speaking globally, that formerly baptism preceded the total Christian initiation (one need only think, for example, of the practice of infant baptism). It was administered after a run-through on the doctrine of the Church. This was fairly stereotyped, just as the rite of baptism which always had the same invariable form. This came from a one-sided understanding of the power of salvation emanating from baptism and the reduction of the Gospel to a resume of the doctrine of the Church in the form of questions and answers. In contemporary practice we find an ever increasing harmonization between baptism and catechesis and the desire to adapt evangelization to different ages and cultures, in order to do more justice to the Good News, as well as to embrace the whole life of the catechumen. These are the same tendencies that are treated in thematic fashion in the other contributions of this volume and thus gain in immediate interest, thanks to the concrete information this sounding of the Church throughout the world has given us.

M. C. VANHENGEL, O.P.
Secretary General

J. PETERS, O.C.D.
Assistant Secretary

FRANCE

"In view of the frequent apostasy of Christians in our time, it may be that the Church will come to reserve baptism only for children whose families are truly Christian and offer a genuine opportunity for a religious education; whereas, in the case of others, it will reintroduce adult baptism, thus giving back to this sacrament, for those who would receive it at the age of reason, its full significance." [1]

A monk, Dom Cabrol, wrote those lines in 1906, pointing the way to the renewal of the catechumenate in France.

In fact the birth of the Catechumenal Institute is due to a number of influences: historical research on the catechumenate, the rediscovery of adult conversion, the desire for a dialogue with non-Christians, the missionary concern to meet men in their lives and, finally, the desire to link personal baptism with the collective life of the Church. Both historians and theologians thus join with pastors in the field of practical pastoral work.

Let us first try briefly to sum up this development; then we will examine the ways in which the Catechumenal Institute manifests itself within the pastoral scene in the mission of the Church of France; finally, we will raise a few contemporary problems.

Toward an Organized Catechumenate

In France, which was by definition a Christian country, one had not imagined that adults could be non-believers. Consequently, one did not put great emphasis on the conversion of those who presented themselves for baptism. Whether the conversion was complete or not, it was feared that by making this an important issue, one would begin to believe that France was no longer Christian, that the Church was losing ground. Consequently, the whole preparation for baptism and the celebration itself took place in a climate of extreme discretion. It was always a kind of review course for the candidate. Moreover, people

[1] F. Cabrol, *Les origines liturgiques* (Paris, 1906), p. 168.

generally thought that, once baptized, adults would become naturally Christian, since they wanted it.

An unexpected event changed this point of view. It happened that several conversions attracted a great deal of attention: for example, the conversion in 1912 of Renan's grandson, Ernest Psichari, who, in the eyes of many, belonged to the group called the *"méchants"*. Indeed, the attention given to these conversions resembled that given to film stars today. But gradually people of various backgrounds came into the Church and their step seemed an honest one.

From 1930 there was a great missionary movement in France. The slogan was: "We must make our brothers Christians again." [2] If this slogan contained the idea of conquest, there was also a desire to reach the masses slowly, by degrees, avoiding what was called fishing with a hook—that is, the conversion of an isolated adult who, by coming into the Church, cut himself off from his milieu. Consequently, the concern was more and more to set a whole group moving, starting with one adult who found faith and attached himself to Christ. In the amazing book by Abbé Godin, *France, pays de mission,* a work that has had considerable missionary influence for the last twenty years, one finds in many places the idea and even the word "catechumenate".[3]

Not until the year 1950 or 1952, however, was there sufficient official awareness of the situation, and definite efforts were undertaken to welcome adults asking for baptism. The cardinal of Lyons was responsible for the first directive reestablishing the catechumenate.[4] The idea was launched, and in Paris various efforts were soon combined, while gradually in the other dioceses,

---

[2] The birth of the J.O.C. A well-known hymn of the time:
  To make once more our brothers Christian
  By Jesus Christ we swear,
  And the light and flame by which we burn
  To them we seek to bear.

[3] H. Godin and Y. Daniel, *France, pays de mission.* Rencontres 12 (Lyons, 1943).

[4] The instruction "Semaine Religieuse" (Lyons: November 6, 1953). Abbé Cellier is named the responsible diocesan appointee.

as in Paris, diocesan appointees were made responsible for the whole undertaking.

The Decree of the Congregation of Rites (April 16, 1962) caused the majority of bishops to institute a catechumenate, forestalling the decisions of the Council.[5] When they wrote their directive, the following words expressed their awareness: ". . . responsible for the celebration of adult baptism and concerned to supervise the preparation of every adult catechumen for the sacraments of Christian initiation (baptism, confirmation and the eucharist), in conformity with the tradition of the Church." [6] However, the responsible people in each diocese already knew one another and worked together within the apostolic regions set aside by the episcopate.[7] The Episcopal Commission of Religious Instruction, which is concerned with promoting the catechumenal pastorate, created in 1964 a national service to coordinate pastoral research and activate it in conjunction with all the other vital forces of the Church.[8]

What Is the Actual Work of the Catechumenal Institute within the Pastorate?

Let us try to sum up the work so far and point out its influence within the Church. The work of the catechumenate is grouped under three headings: sponsorship, catechesis, liturgy.

1. *The Work of Sponsorship.* In regard to sponsorship, work is most difficult. It has been clear from the beginning that catechumens would have a great deal of difficulty in depending on Christians for their progress. Those who took part in the

[5] *Decree on the Pastoral Office of Bishops in the Church.*

[6] This standard directive, the first words of which we quote, was proposed to the bishops by the Episcopal Commissions on Liturgy and Religious Instruction.

[7] It is necessary to note the publication of a special number of the review Catéchèse: "Problèmes de Catéchuménat" whose editor was Abbé Coudreau, one of the principal initiators of catechumenal work in France. He is the responsible diocesan in Paris.

[8] The National Service, directly dependent on the Episcopal Commission responsible for promoting the Catechumenal Pastorate, has its Secretariat at 37 rue Linné, Paris 5e. It has a documents service, a quarterly bulletin of information and observations, and information sheets for nuns.

national assembly at Blois in 1962, just at the moment when all the dioceses were organizing a serious catechumenal effort, noted that there was a very low rate of perseverance.[9]

With this severe view in mind, the problem of the welcome to catechumens was reconsidered, and the question of the time necessary for a proper catechumenate was raised once again. It soon became clear that sponsorship was the key, or, at any rate, one of the keys to success. It was soon apparent that it was not enough to allot one sponsor to a catechumen. It was necessary to find in the catechumen's background people who could help him a little in his progress. Natural bonds were sought that would help to set the conversion within a milieu. In short, the accent was placed far more on this collective aspect of sponsorship than on its individual aspect. This awareness of considerable and fruitful work was responsible for an increase in the percentage of those persevering.[10]

Sponsorship became more and more clearly understood in the minds of those responsible for this new approach. The national assembly of 1964 was the occasion of more profound insight in this field. Conversion no longer appeared as an individual phenomenon but as a growth within a milieu, within the people who comprise the Church, within grace that the Holy Spirit has also given outside the Church. In their own experiences, those responsible rediscovered what Abbé Dujarier[11] had shown in regard to what had taken place in the first centuries and what the conciliar texts[12] have again told us: the whole Church must exercise a sponsoring function, and it is naturally the task of sponsors to stimulate conversions.

Assigning sponsorship its proper role becomes the primary concern in welcoming those adults who come for baptism with-

[9] Under present conditions, taking account of the difficulties of estimating numbers, 20% has been named as the number of those persevering, as with children.

[10] Some recent samplings suggest that the number of those who persevere is now in the region of 80%.

[11] P. Dujarier, *Le parrainage des adultes aux trois premiers siècles* (Paris: Ed. du Cerf).

[12] For example, the *Decree on the Church's Missionary Activity* (n. 14).

out being converted, and there are many of them. A large number of eventual catechumens come to the Church because of marriage, but they ask for the sacrament without faith. Consequently, this period is not, strictly speaking, the province of the catechumenate, although it functions as a substitute. We shall note a difficulty on this point at the end of this article.

2. *Large Number of Catechists.* Catechesis was a constant concern of the catechumenate. Many considered that the problem of preparing adults for the sacraments of Christian initiation had to be resolved by adapted instruction. Undoubtedly this is why the Episcopal Commission on Religious Instruction and the National Center of Religious Instruction created in 1956 a subcommission for the catechesis of adult catechumens, which combined theologians, catechists,[13] pastors and members of the Higher Institute of the Catechetical Pastorate. This subcommission would train catechists to meet existing needs, for the catechumens were relatively numerous in relation to the priests available. Great interest was shown by nuns, whose influence in the development of the catechumenate in France should be noted. A large number of lay people also showed interest.

In the large cities, a number of evening courses[14] resembling a miniature university aroused great interest. Thus, in the Paris region, thousands of people received catechetical training; furthermore, there was a great upsurge of questions and research on the part of both students and teachers. Courses attended by groups of catechists tended to become true centers of reflection, a kind of permanent workshop. In offering themselves as catechists, some generous Christians thought they would be useful; at the same time they were hoping to receive instruction themselves. They became men and women more sensitive to the quest for their brethren, more attentive to dialogue and its contents, and they worked to make that part of the Church with which they were in contact more aware. The training of cate-

[13] We may note the names of Père Liégé and H. Denis (theologians), and of the Abbés Saudreau, Coudreau and Cellier.

[14] Some courses have had a considerable influence, like those of Abbé Coudreau. They have been published.

chists is easier in towns than in rural milieux. Priests, nuns and laymen would swell the number of catechists for adults if we had the time and the means to train them.

Every catechist gradually comes to discover the dual problem the Church has to resolve: how to approach the dialogue about God and how to give faith an adult form in a specific culture.

These courses opened a new approach to pastoral theology. It was a matter not only of illuminating for the first time a growing faith, but also of nourishing this faith as it grew in order to give it an intellectual framework which satisfied the adult mind. Research at all levels is done in close connection with the work of the catechesis of adults and under the aegis of those whom the episcopate has made responsible. At all levels, those in charge of catechesis must feel themselves just as responsible for the catechesis of catechumens and also for the training of catechists. The catechesis of adults is certainly starting to hold a place in the minds of bishops and priests that it has never had.[15]

3. *The Catechumenal Liturgy.* The Decree of the Congregation of Rites opens up a new perspective in liturgy.[16] As an experiment, certain bishops were already welcoming catechumens in a series of successive stages. These were, in particular: (1) the rite of the entry into the catechumenate, which opened the period (of greater or lesser length) of the catechumenate itself; (2) the time of the final preparation for baptism.

Each of these periods is preceded by a choice that is incorporated in the liturgy. The place of the liturgy in catechumenal work was not always appreciated by those who were bringing adults to baptism. The rites seem to be more an illustration of catechesis than an intervention of God within the life of men. However, a certain number of catechumenates[17] did deepen re-

[15] The National Service publishes documents.

[16] Abbé Chavasse in *Problèmes de Catéchuménat*, pp. 87-101.

[17] A special number of *Maison-Dieu*, n. 71: "Catéchuménat et Liturgie"; A. Laurentin, "Le Nouveau Rituel du Baptême," in *Paroisse et Liturgie*, January 1, 1963; Coudreau et Feder, *Rituel du Baptême* (Paris: Ed. Mame).

search into the liturgy. They placed it better within the whole framework of catechumenal preparation and experimented seriously with the celebration of the Word and the rites of Christian initiation, proving that liturgy is truly at the heart of the catechumenate and that it is the meeting of God and man. The emphasis on the celebration of the Word for the catechumenate reinforced in this field the work of liturgical reform.

Actually, the rite of entry is considered as the real rite of initial conversion and of effective entry into the Church. This opens the catechumenal period, properly speaking, in which the ripening of faith is undertaken experimentally. This period, more and more serious, becomes long enough for the apprenticeship to the Christian life to be made with every chance of perseverance. With the approach of Lent, if the catechumens strongly desire it and are considered suitable, there is the great baptismal retreat. Often, at the beginning of Lent, *at the request of the bishop*,[18] who thus shows his responsibility, those who are to be baptized are called together in order to begin this final preparation. These "elect of God" join in the paschal vigil after rites marking the intervention of the Church (scrutinies and traditions).

Through this whole approach to baptism the catechumenate endeavors to place within a limited framework several crucial problems of which it is necessary to speak. We are going through a kind of crisis in the rite, caused partly by the catechumenate itself. Several rites raise real difficulties, but beyond these difficulties the deeper question is posed as to the appropriateness of our rites in general to the contemporary world. The catechumenate is a privileged group, a group of new believers who are particularly sensitive to this problem.

The Effect of the Catechumenate

All these efforts in the field of sponsorship, catechesis and liturgy have obviously had an effect on the life of the Church

[18] In the provinces the bishop is often able to participate in the catechumenal liturgy. In Paris he assembles once a year all the catechumens who are starting the baptismal retreat.

itself. The catechumenate was welcomed as the response of the Church to those adults in search of dialogue with a view to baptism or to entry into the eucharistic life of the Church. The elements of Christian initiation that the diocesan appointee was charged with introducing were accepted by many, especially the need for conversion and the time factor. The place of the laity was also recognized, not because they could be useful but because people gradually realized that the whole Church had to welcome catechumens. In this welcome the laity had a predominant role. Just as, on the occasion of a newborn son, it was necessary to coordinate not only catechumenal functions but also those of the Church, the catechumenate became rather like the spur of the pastorate.

The field in which it has raised perhaps the most important questions is that of faith and the sacraments. Bishop Garronne stated in 1963 that the catechumenate was a phenomenon that would have great influence within the Church. The seriousness with which catechumens are treated and the lightness with which infant baptism and marriages are accepted without faith appear contradictory. Therefore, the reexamination of all our attitudes becomes inevitable.

"Thanks to the catechumenate," says Bishop Maziers, "we are led to examine ourselves, both at the level of individuals and of institutions, on the way in which we are a sign and a call to those who are seeking God." In a document from the Pastoral Secretariat of the Episcopate one reads: "The conversion of a single adult who passes from unbelief to faith has a prophetic character for the Church and for the world: it is a sign of the march toward the salvation of a whole group of men and of their welcome which has already begun in the Church of Jesus Christ."

Conclusions

Catechumenal work has not been placed sufficiently within the total pastoral situation. Too many priests transfer their responsibilities "to those who, in their field, are thought to repre-

sent catechumenal work". Furthermore, the welcome to catechumens and, above all, to those who come and are not converted is sometimes criticized by the most missionary elements
of the Church. It is to be feared that the milieu that should support the process of conversion does not exist, and that the
catechumenate is artificially restoring something that must appear in a more natural form from the beginning. The catechumenate shares this preoccupation, but it is faced with a problem
it cannot resolve. As we deepen the relation that exists with
missionary work and think of the catechumenate rather than of
a total pastorate,[19] our efforts will be linked with evangelization.
The catechumenate must become part of the missionary work of
the Church.

Present research on a national level, as we move toward the
promulgation of a new ritual that will fulfill the desires of all,
is being undertaken in two directions: (1) the study of the
phenomenon of conversions by specialists who will look at it
from a fresh point of view; (2) the examination of the criteria
of conversion used by the authorities responsible for the catechumenate. Then, as pastors and theologians we will be able to
learn the appropriate lessons and bring to the contemporary
Church, which is engaged in self-examination concerning the
discussion with the adult unbeliever, a little more hope and joy,
for salvation has come.

BERNARD GUILLARD

SPAIN

The Spanish Church is undoubtedly more established than
missionary. Most of those responsible for pastoral action still

---

[19] On condition that the total pastorate is not merely a coordination
of efforts, but an attempt to place the Church in a missionary state.

seem to be living in the belief that there is an almost complete equation between the number of Spaniards and the number of Catholics whose faith is proof against anything (even though often not all that highly developed), and that the traditional pastoral methods and institutions are still adequate for Spain. In this climate of opinion, it is hardly surprising that missionary-inspired initiatives have not exactly proliferated.

Nevertheless, the last thirty years have not been devoid of realists who have denounced the grave failings of the religious state of the country. The emergence of religious sociology has backed them up to a degree that no one suspected.

There is now a very live missionary preoccupation in some sectors of the clergy and laity, and some interesting ideas are being put into practice. Documentation on these is still scarce, but I will try to give as complete a picture as possible of what is being done in the fields of evangelization and the catechumenate.

I

THE SOCIO-RELIGIOUS SITUATION IN SPAIN

Missionary pastoral activity is necessary to a greater or lesser extent depending on the religious situation of a country. It cannot be claimed that, in the case of Spain, this is known with any degree of precision. The last years have, somewhat later than in other European countries, produced an awakening of interest in religious sociology,[1] although the picture of Spanish religion is still far too incomplete.[2] Some aspects of direct concern to the present subject have still not been studied at all, but there are enough scraps of information to show that the

[1] Cf. P. Almerich, "The Present Position of Religious Sociology in Spain," in *Social Compass* 12 (1965), pp. 312-20.
[2] There is a good summary of what has been done so far in R. Duocastella, "Géographie de la pratique religieuse en Espagne," *ibid.*, pp. 253-302.

situation cries out for the renewal of present-day pastoral methods and institutions.

Spain, one must remember, "is a country of great contrasts: socio-economic, cultural, political, historical and, consequently, religious".[3] Thus, if the picture painted here seems a very negative one, it should not be forgotten that there are large areas of Spain where the practice of religion is at a very high level by almost any standards.

Our generation has seen a radical change of attitude with regard to infant baptism in regions considered de-Christianized. Fr. Sarabia summed up the situation before the Civil War in these terms: "There are towns in many parts of Spain where a large proportion of the children are not baptized. In the outer suburbs of Madrid, this proportion reaches 25%, and in the working-class quarters of Barcelona there are thousands who have refused baptism. In the mining regions of Asturias, Extremadura, Andalusia . . . almost half the children are unbaptized." [4] Today the vast majority of parents in these same regions have their children baptized. But this change is largely due to social pressure, due to the privileged position that the Church enjoys in Spain today.

The pattern of religious education of children is extremely mixed. Two examples, one from a large industrial city and one from a rural area, can be taken to illustrate the lowest end of the scale. In the seven main suburban areas of Barcelona, with a population of 161,800, 62% of the children do not learn the catechism.[5] In the archpriesthood of Ocera, in the diocese of Jaen, only 3.4% of the total population receives regular religious ministration; a further 6.8% has access to Mass two or three Sundays every month, 40% once or twice a year, and the remainder—just about 50%—absolutely nothing.[6] The situation

[3] *Ibid.*, p. 257.

[4] *¿Espana. . . . es católica?* (Madrid, 1939), p. 45.

[5] Cf. J. Sola, "Sociología religiosa urbana y misiones parroquiales," in *Razón y Fe* 161 (1960), p. 30; R. Duocastella, *Los suburbios de Barcelona* (Barcelona, 1957).

[6] Cf. R. Duocastella, *op. cit. supra*, footnote 2.

could be paralleled in remote parts of the provinces of Seville, Badajoz and Cáceres, the plain of Nijar in Almería and other districts in the province of Jaen.[7]

The religious education of children is reflected in an interesting way in the numbers of National Servicemen (enlisted men) who make their first communion every year in the barracks. According to the official bulletin of the "Ecclesiastical Jurisdiction for Military Camps", there were 9,498 first communions in 1944; 15,000 in 1945; 11,839 in 1947; 12,492 in 1949; 13,354 in 1950; 11,839 in 1951; 9,863 in 1952; 8,541 in 1953; 8,745 in 1955; 6,719 in 1956; 6,425 in 1958; 7,006 in 1959; 5,428 in 1960; 3,551 in 1961; 2,874 in 1962; 2,852 in 1963; 2,298 in 1964 and 2,838 in 1965. The steadily declining numbers indicate a general improvement in catechesis throughout the whole country.

Surveys on Sunday Mass attendance indicate vast masses of baptized Catholics who live on the fringe of any direct influence of the Church. More than 90% of the population of the provinces of Andalusia, Alicante and Valencia, for example, do not go to Mass on Sundays.[8] Among the working classes, a very high percentage (89.6%) declare themselves to be anti-clerical and a relatively high percentage (41.3%) anti-religious.[9] The religious problems of industrial regions have been further complicated by the high proportion of migrant workers.[10]

Besides the numbers of non-practicing Catholics, the Protestants in Spain are a tiny minority. Figures supplied by pastors of the major groups indicate that the Spanish Reformed Episcopal Church has between 1,500 and 2,000 members, the Spanish

[7] Cf. J. Azpiazu, "¿De dónde nace la irreligiosidad de las masas trabajadores en España?" in *Fomento Social* 4 (1949), p. 270.

[8] R. Duocastella, *op. cit.*, pp. 276-85, has collected all the data known until now on Sunday Mass attendance in different parts of Spain.

[9] Cf. A. Conin, "L'Espagne, pays de mission. La jeunesse ouvrière et l'Eglise," in *Esprit* (Feb. 1964), p. 317; R. Duocastella, *op. cit.*, p. 301.

[10] Cf. R. Duocastella, "Estudio de las migraciones internas en España," in *Documentación Social* (Madrid, 1958), p. 4.

Evangelical Baptist Union about 6,000 and the Spanish Evangelical Church about 10,000.[11]

II

SIGNS OF PASTORAL RENEWAL

Pastoral institutions and methods generally reflect a concept of Spain as a thoroughly Christian country with no great missionary problems. At the same time, the idea that missionary activity is needed is gaining ground. The appearance in the last few years of two journals reflecting this point of view, *Pentecostes* and *Pastoral Misionera,* is an indication of this.

However, there is still no diocese with an organization for missionary pastoral work at the diocesan level. One can only talk of missionary tendencies finding their way into already existing apostolic organizations or giving rise to new institutions. There has been for some years now, for example, a strong movement of catechetical renewal, well-organized by a central body, which runs various Institutes at national and diocesan levels. This is beginning to make its influence felt on the general level of Spanish religious education.

The People's Missions, which have had such an influence on the religious life of the country, are presently going through a phase of revising their methods and trying to adapt their message more to the present lines of missionary pastoral activity.[12] The "Obra de Ejercicios" (Spiritual Exercises Group) has for several years been organizing special courses for de-Christianized working-class areas. The "Cursillos de Cristianidad" (Short Courses of Christianity) have brought a new apostolic and missionary awareness wherever they have been held.[13]

A missionary orientation has been steadily more noticeable

[11] Cf. N. Vall, "Encuesta dirigida a las comunidades protestantes españolas," in *Unitas* 5 (1966), pp. 36-37.
[12] Cf. M. Vidal, "La Misión Parroquial, hoy," in *Pentecostes* 10 (1966), pp. 113-33.
[13] Cf. J. Hervas, "Los Cursillos de Cristiandad," in *Cristo al mundo* (1962), pp. 171-90, 337-51.

in the different groups of Catholic Action, particularly in those specializing in the working-class mission. In the last twenty years the "Diocesan Missionary Priests" from dioceses with an ample supply of clergy have established themselves in some regions in the south where there has long been a shortage of priests. "Fe católica" and "Casa de la Biblia" are effectively promoting biblical education through study weeks, study groups and radio broadcasts.

In 1965 a year's adult catechumenate course was started in the Moratalaz district of Madrid. Inspired by the great tradition of the early Church, its aim is to develop an adult faith in practicing Christians whose religious education has serious deficiencies. This experiment was undertaken as a first step toward a permanent institution at diocesan level. The Pastoral Institute has also organized a similar course in one of the University Colleges.

III

ADULT BAPTISM

The twenty-eight replies I received to a circular inquiry about the number of adults baptized in each diocese in the last years indicate that in some dioceses—such as Cuenca, Cuidad Real, Segovia, Vitoria, Granada, Zamora, Zaragoza and several smaller ones—there are hardly any—two, three or four a year —whereas in others the numbers are quite high, at least a few dozen a year, reaching three figures in Valencia (233, 231, 260, 166, 180), Barcelona ("several hundred each year") and Madrid (411, 403, 408, 423, 383). These figures do not include the number of National Servicemen (enlisted men) baptized each year: usually between 100 and 200 each year from 1953 to 1962, rising to 287 in 1964 and falling to 55 in 1965.

To my knowledge there is no diocesan organization in charge of preparing candidates for baptism. This is usually done entirely by private initiative. "Fe católica" in Madrid uses trained laymen who have instructed 245 candidates, most of them foreigners, since 1956.

The sacrament itself is usually administered privately, without involving the parish community, except for the rather exceptional cases where candidates are baptized during the Easter Vigil service. The new "Ordo" which allows for the catechumenate to be divided into different liturgical phases is even less frequently used.

A situation like this clearly calls for the establishment of new "Catechumenate Centers" in those dioceses where the number of adult baptisms is fairly high.[14] There is, in fact, a movement to establish such a center in Madrid. The same is true of the military barracks; it would not seem impossible in the present circumstances to think of gathering all the recruits from one draft who ask to be baptized into one place where they could all be instructed together.

But the vast mass of those who are baptized and then never receive any religious instruction—or, if they do, on an entirely inadequate level—presents an even graver pastoral problem. It is widely being said that Spain is a sacramentalized country but not an evangelized one. The task should not be left entirely to private initiative. The pastoral institutions of each diocese should find an important place in their work for evangelizing activity directed toward those who have no religion, and for catechesis on the level of a catechumenate for those adults who are more or less practicing Christians but who have never undergone any genuine Christian initiation. Adult confirmations, and marriage preparation courses in particular, could well become the ground for a sort of disguised catechumenate. In dioceses where the number of adult candidates for baptism is small, these could also benefit from this sort of catechumenate. The meetings of the "Cursillos" in Ultreya[15] could also evolve toward the stimulation of this important missionary activity.

IGNACIO OÑATIBIA

---

[14] Cf. J. Totosaus, "Problemas actuales de catequesis," in *Phase* 5 (1965), pp. 139-46.

[15] Cf. C. Floristán, "Los Cursillos de cristiandad y el catecumenado," in *Incunable* (May, 1961).

LATIN AMERICA

The question with which any discussion of the catechumenate in Latin America must start is whether any form of catechumenate really can be said to exist on this continent. The results of one research would seem to indicate that at the time of writing (June, 1966) it does not, in any meaningful sense. There are certain things—generally the result of individual initiative—which might be laying the foundations for a future catechumenate, such as the activities of the Salesian missionaries in Ecuador, but there is nothing official or widespread.

The most important experiment being made is undoubtedly a cooperative venture by seven parishes in the archdiocese of Buenos Aires. The priests of these parishes have grouped together to organize a course of instruction for those adults who come to them asking to be baptized or confirmed, to make their first communion or get married. One of the parish priests is in charge of the course. The experiment was only started in July, 1965; therefore, it is too early yet to judge how lasting its results are.

No adult is baptized until after a year's catechumenate. If one of the partners asking to get married is not yet baptized, the priest obtains a dispensation for a mixed marriage, witnesses the marriage and then starts a year's course of instruction before the person concerned is baptized. The general principle is that the sacraments are not given in a hurry and it is made quite clear to those who ask for them that they will be given as soon as they are completely prepared for their reception.

Great importance is attached to personal contact between the catechumen and the priest, first as a contact in brotherly love, and later to ensure a more complete assimilation of the teaching on the sacrament to be received, as well as in individual adaptation to its demands, according to the recipient's age, sex, cultural level and response to the Gospel message. Those catechumens close to each other in general culture and development also meet in groups, and there are also general inter-parochial

gatherings, joint celebrations of the Liturgy of the Word, re-
treats and social activities.

This experiment, though the most noteworthy, is not the only
one that holds the seeds of a future widespread catechumenate.
The Catechetical Center of the archdiocese of Mexico has prepared a schema, and there is much work being done on the missions. The starting point has been the realization that the sacramental life by itself is insufficient; it must have a strong basis
of faith and the Gospel message. This conviction that real preparation for the sacraments is a duty of conscience has come as
a result of a new appreciation of what the Church in the modern
world must be. It is of no use simply to look for a numerical
increase in baptisms if baptism is not followed by a real life of
faith; it is not enough to frequent the sacraments if these sacraments are not a witness to, and profession of, this same faith to
the Church and to the world.

The people of Latin America are still generally religious in
their own way, and their religiosity has a Christian origin: the
people receive the sacraments and practice a host of different
devotions. Where these devotions are lacking, their religiosity
will show itself in pseudo-Christian or completely superstitious
beliefs. This general religiosity, taken with the genuine faith of
small minorities who still act as the leaven in the dough, gives
the impression of a viable Christianity, a living Church. The result is a haze of general drowsiness through which it is impossible
to see the need for change, the need to *want* to improve things
even if this improvement must involve a break in the routine,
the changing of many traditions, new elements and practices in
pastoral work, and even restrictions placed on some aspects of
the sacramental life.

This special climate of Latin American religion is not exactly
favorable to an imminent implantation of the catechumenate,
and there are no sure signs that it will change in the immediate
future. People's consciences are still not sufficiently awake. The
Gospel-Church problem gives rise to a certain anxiety, but not
enough thought is given to it. There is still a general impression

that the traditional pastoral methods are the only safe ones and so cannot be changed; therefore, the routine goes on. There is also a feeling of insecurity when pastoral changes designed to accord with the demands of real faith are introduced. This attitude, which fortunately is now giving ground fairly widely, leads to a reaction against the "new-fangled ideas" of those who try to set more demanding standards for the faith required before the sacraments are administered. It confirms some in their traditional methods and in others encourages immobilism, routine and often downright laziness.

The catechumenate for adults, enjoined by the *Constitution on the Sacred Liturgy* (n. 64) needs to be restored in Latin America, too. This would be a prerequisite for parents (and possibly godparents as well) who bring their children to be baptized when their own lives are not a witness to the faith in the community in which they live. It would also be required for those who wish to sanctify their mutual love and make it a sign of the union between Christ and his Church. The sacraments of baptism and confirmation could also be the occasions for other forms of catechumenate, both for those who are going to receive the sacrament and for their parents.

A catechumenate such as this would have to be organized on a diocesan level, in order to avoid the situation in which those who were told that they had to undergo instruction before receiving a sacrament in one parish would merely go to a neighboring parish in which this requirement was not in force. It would also have to be more than just a "catechism class" devoid of conviction, dialogue, personal contact in brotherly love and adaptation to the needs of each individual and each particular sacrament.

There are several relevant questions to be asked on the subject. Do the young clergy consider Latin America evangelized or not? The results of one inquiry suggest that it is not only the progressives but the young clergy as a whole who find their pastoral work seriously hindered. They find that devotional practices are widespread, and often that the sacraments are frequented, but that there is seldom any genuine life of faith, any living, personal adherence to the Gospel. The people are baptized, but most of them know nothing about the mystery of salvation or the primacy of charity in the life of faith. The clergy's hands are tied by this devotional sort of religion because their very livelihood usually depends on it. When, on the grounds of sound theology, they try to curb certain excesses, they are not always understood and their efforts tend to be condemned under the blanket heading of "innovations".

Is the Church really devoting herself to her basic task of evangelization? Many of those who replied to the inquiry considered that the Church was taking a more active part in the solution of social problems and in the fields of secondary and university education for the relatively wealthy. Organizations such as CLAF (The Latin American Committee of the Faith, a division of CELAM) and the CDC are doing good catechetical work, but their influence, too, is very limited in comparison with the scale of the problem—the masses who are still in need of thorough evangelization and basic catechetics.

There are groups of priests who understand the urgency of restoring the catechumenate for adults in the spirit of the Constitution, but again they are few and far between. Only a small proportion of the clergy have been able to attend recent courses of pastoral action, catechetics or liturgy in order to rid themselves of outdated formulas or institutions that prevent the implantation of the Gospel or at least make it difficult. There are also courses of preparation for marriage, most of them organized by the MFC (Family Christian Movement), but they are not yet ideal in themselves and again can only reach a small minority of the people.

The hopes of the Church in Latin America are placed in the national hierarchies. The faithful are waiting for the Episcopal Conferences to implement the Council decisions. Some Conferences have already produced plans for immediate or long-term action, inspired by the Constitutions and Decrees of Vatican Council II and elaborated by experts drawn from both clergy and laity, such as the national pastoral plans of Brazil, Chile and Ecuador. Latin America is opening its eyes to the momentous times through which it is passing and one must hope that this will produce a flourishing Church for the future.

JAIRO MEJÍA GOMEZ

JAPAN

Missionary work in Japan has always been difficult because of the unique situation the Church has always faced there. From the beginning of evangelization four hundred years ago, and even with the revival of missionary work during this past century, Christian missionaries in Japan have continually been confronted with the discouraging reality of a self-sufficient culture which feels no need for Christianity. Unlike many other parts of the world, where Christian teaching and human culture arrived hand-in-hand, Japanese culture was already highly developed by the time the first missionaries arrived in the 16th century. Even in modern times, the Japanese regard their cultural and social progress as something totally independent of Christian influence.

What the Japanese tend to overlook is the fact that the contemporary progress of mankind toward democratic society and refined social structures is rooted in an undercurrent of religious values introduced into the flow of human history by Christ himself. The developing culture of the world, which has taken its direction from the Christianized culture of the West, is rooted in the grace of God reshaping human history into the image of Christ. Christ has been at work in his Church to cast light on authentic human values and guide the inner dynamism of human history. Thus, modern man cannot but be affected by the saving act of Christ, cannot but meet the salvific influence of the Church in human culture. But the Japanese do not realize that the contemporary cultural advance is something basically owing to Christ, to God. They see it as a process taking place independently of Christianity, and they will recognize the social significance of the Christian Church only insofar as it makes some positive contribution of its own, like any other social group, toward this common cultural advance.

The Japanese have abundant contact with the cultural products of Christianity. For instance, in the home of an average Japanese intellectual, along with the usual Shinto or Buddhist shrine, there might well be some famous painting of the Blessed Virgin or various recordings of sacred music. The major Christian classics have been translated and are well known. The bible, among the foremost of the best-sellers in Japan, is widely read as one of the world's great books. Other contacts with Christianity, direct and indirect, are made through the mass media, through Christian educational institutions and the various organs of Christian social welfare. Thus, since the Japanese arrive at their knowledge of Christianity in such a great variety of fragmentary ways—usually from the outside, as it were—it is only natural that there should also be great variety, and even opposition, in their evaluations of Christianity as a cultural phenomenon. Such variety and opposition, moreover, are manifest not only in their knowledge and objective evaluation of Christianity, but also, of course, in their subjective attitudes and feelings toward it.

Since such is the field where the seed of the Gospel must be planted, it goes without saying that evangelization must be preceded by some sort of *pre-evangelization,* as it has come to be called—a period of preparation during which the individual is brought into contact with Christianity in such a way as to enable him to form a more adequate picture of what Christianity really is. This period, naturally enough, varies in duration, content and method, according to the psychological state of the individual concerned. Therefore, it is not because the prospective convert in Japan is ignorant of Christianity that he needs this period of pre-evangelization, but rather because the fragmentary

knowledge of Christianity which he has picked up from his reading and his daily life, along with the overall impression he may
have received from various Christians and their Churches, has
left him with an attitude toward Christianity which, through no
fault of his own, is filled with misunderstandings, prejudices and,
in many instances, extravagant expectations.

Pre-evangelization, then, demands that the missionary should
focus his attention on the individual, listening to him and understanding him. This attitude must, of course, be maintained
throughout all the phases of missionary work. However, *evangelization in the proper sense* focuses more directly on the amazing message of salvation brought by Christ and fulfilled in the
Christian. The demands of evangelization are exacting: the
Word of God allows of no distortion or compromise, no hesitation or diffidence.

Nevertheless, the temptations to diffidence and distortion are
acute in a country like Japan if the missionary is not careful to
distinguish pre-evangelization from evangelization. When one
attempts to sow the seed before preparing the field, one is easily
tempted to modify and compromise the Christian message itself.
When one presents the Gospel only to find that people do not
accept it, there is danger that he will lose confidence in speaking
directly of supernatural realities and will end up reducing faith
to a natural phenomenon. When this happens, the impression is
easily conveyed that Christianity is simply equivalent to a "nat-
ural-law morality" or some special type of "world view". As
a result, people do not feel urged to take the daring step toward
true conversion. At the heart of the Christian message is the
Word of God, allowing of no distortion and bearing within itself
the power to move men toward a total commitment to God, if
only this Word is given the power, through the work of evangelization, to reach men today.

In Japan, at present, the basic distinction between pre-evangelization and evangelization is, unfortunately, not yet clearly
carried out in practice. Therefore, one cannot isolate and evaluate kerygmatic preaching as a missionary method in Japan today.

On the other hand, many feel that missionary procedure now practiced there does not exert the impact needed to urge prospective converts to overcome their inertia and make the Christian commitment. The reason is that the "conversion point" is generally ignored in theory and thus also in practice. Either the proper time for urging conversion is allowed to pass by unheeded, or else catechetical instruction is introduced and carried on as an academic pursuit, something to be "given" and "heard".

The problem involved in discerning conversion and beginning *the catechumenate* is that different people are ready to enter the catechumenate at different times. The difficulty this poses is especially evident when there is question of group instruction— except perhaps for students in schools, who tend to move forward together at a rather uniform pace. Missionaries in Japan do not agree as to what the conditions should be for entry into the catechumenate. Therefore, since the notion and practice of the catechumenate in Japan is very fluid, it is impossible to offer any figures as to its duration. In general, however, it is safe to say that once a person begins to receive regular weekly instructions, it generally takes from six months to a year until baptism.

Faith, of course, is a gift and cannot be said to depend solely on *catechetical methods*. But most missionaries realize that the fine catechisms designed for use in the Christian countries are quite unsuitable for use in a missionary country. The European catechetical revival, along with the experience of missionary difficulties in Japan, led, some ten or more years ago, to a call for a Christ-centered catechetical renewal in Japan too. The catechism sponsored by the Japanese hierarchy has not yet embodied this renewal. No partial revision can any longer meet the need; radical renovation is imperative. Reform of the catechumenate depends to a great extent on such a catechetical renovation.

The reform of the catechumenate also depends on *liturgical renovation*. Surely, the preaching of the Good News of Christ must come first, urging people to commit themselves to Christ. But once the basic conversion and commitment to Christ have been achieved, the convert has to be brought into living contact with the living Church: he must be led to prayer and to association with baptized Christians. As suggested in the *Constitution on the Sacred Liturgy,* a restoration of the liturgy for catechumens will help toward this purpose. The formal liturgical acceptance of the baptismal candidates into the Church, the introduction of the sponsors and the forging of bonds between the new believers and the body of the Church are all very meaningful for the Christian initiation of converts.

Scripture services, built around the catechetical themes, should be used to lead the new Christian to a liturgical experience of God's Word so that the knowledge acquired in the instructions may penetrate more deeply into the heart, and that the Christian may thus be led to live the mysteries of salvation in union with Christ (*mystagogia*). Nourished, through the liturgy, on the Word of God in scripture and eventually in the sacraments, the Christian is brought into living contact with the living Christ.

The missionary needs a kerygmatic and pastoral theological synthesis from which to work—a basically scriptural curriculum integrating the doctrinal and moral catechesis he must impart. It would be an enormous help to the missionary if he had a liturgical integration of all these various elements. A more effective distribution of the scripture readings in the regular Church liturgy, as proposed in the Constitution, is eagerly awaited in the new churches in missionary lands, hungry as they are for the Word of God. If the paschal mystery of Christ is presented as the focal center of the whole history of salvation, retold through relevant scriptural passages distributed over a cycle of several years, while at the same time the outline of the yearly cycle is preserved, then the liturgy will equally serve the Christian formation of all, feeding both new converts and older Christians more effectively with the Word of God.

FRANCIS TSUCHIYA, S.J.

FORMOSA

The evangelization of Formosa has been going on since 1626. In 1949 the life of this little Chinese province was overwhelmed by the arrival of refugees from mainland China. In spite of the grave problems of this situation the country has made great strides in all fields. There has also been a new impetus in the Church, as the following figures will show. In 1945 there were 8,000 Catholics in a population of nearly 8,000,000; in 1965 there were 280,000 Catholics in a population of 12,500,000. There are seven dioceses, of which five are under the authority of Chinese bishops. The proportion of Christians of all denominations is 5%, of which half are Catholics.

The Church is growing all the time. Among the favorable factors, one may note the sympathy and tolerance of the Chinese people toward all religion. There is the search for the meaning of life in face of the suffering of being uprooted and of insecurity. School education has been made possible for all and interest in science and technology are slowly eliminating superstition. In some respects these same elements can become unfavorable factors for Christianity. The welcome given to all religion may result in syncretism; suffering may turn people toward the enjoyment of the accessible goods of this world; wrongly directed scientific knowledge may eliminate all religious sense. Despite the ambiguity of these factors, however, it appears that the majority of conversions have resulted because the efforts of evangelization deepened personal aspirations and led them to their end in Christ.

It is difficult to speak of an organization of the catechumenate because it varies according to place. Religious instruction of the catechumens is done either in groups or individually. It generally takes a minimum of six months, with two or three instructions weekly. In some parishes a course is started as soon as there is a group of interested people, while in others one is able to join a course already in progress and then make up what one has missed in the next course. Sometimes there is instruction that is not only individual but also personal, according to the rhythm of the catechumen and not of the "program". The manual on which the catechumenate is based is generally the traditional catechism. To be admitted to baptism one must pass an examination that covers catechism questions and the recitation of prayers and sometimes includes questions concerning the commitment to a Christian life in the world today. It varies in length according to the time available and the judgment of the priest in charge of the catechumens. There are many conversions everywhere, and apart from general reasons, one may say that the presence and example of Catholic friends or colleagues often have a great influence.

There is much talk of a decrease in the number of conversions over the past years, but the expansion of the Church in Formosa continues; in spite of the growth of population the percentage of Catholics maintains itself and is even growing. It is true that conversions are less spectacular. At the beginning it was necessary to create many new mission posts, but now new Christians must simply integrate themselves into the communities already existing. The large number of refugees have already had an opportunity to take a personal decision concerning the appeal of Christianity. Many aboriginal tribes have been evangelized. After the rapid growth of the spring shoots there follows a slow growth. Nevertheless, it is important to revise the concept of evangelization so as not to limit ourselves to a simple continuation; rather, we must enlarge and deepen it. It is not enough to increase the number of Catholics. Even in this Church which is only at the beginning of her task, we find the sad phenomenon of de-Christianization. Some have been baptized too quickly, for it was considered sufficient to teach the catechism without examining the motives for conversion; this has sometimes resulted in a sociological or utilitarian faith. In these cases a change of external circumstances is enough for people to lose all contact with the Church. In the face of this situation the general tendency at present is to prolong the length of the catechumenate and at the same time to give greater importance to pastoral work among the new Christians. It is desirable and even vital for the Church that everyone should work toward this goal. This presupposes a renewal of the presentation of the Gospel both before and after baptism. For many people this sacrament has been a final point in their religious instruction, instead of being a sacrament of Christian initiation.

It will be necessary to fix a minimum time and criteria for an understanding of Christian life before the admission to baptism of a candidate, and such conditions will have to be observed everywhere. There will also have to be some organization of the catechumenate. Catechumens ought to be introduced to the world of scripture and liturgy not merely by explanations and doctrinal formulas; rather, the whole presentation of the Christian message should be impregnated by it, and liturgical celebrations should be its center. The place of godparents as guides for the neophyte on the way of the Christian life should be emphasized. At the same time the role of the Christian community, awakened to the joy of welcoming new members, should be stressed. Hitherto nothing marked the entry into the catechumenate proper, and even baptism has been in many cases a ceremony separate from the community. The ritual of adult baptism is divided into three stages, but it is still little used; one may hope that it will be reshaped, but it does not correspond to the Chinese mentality anymore than do the other preceding rituals.

A great effort of openness and realism is asked of the workers in the Lord's field in Formosa. It is time to become aware of the situation and to act accordingly. In the history of the Church in China there are some very painful chapters. Today this Church is being tested by persecution. We must not forget our brothers in mainland China who by their suffering are meriting the spring of the Church in the Chinese province of Taiwan. These new Christians must be worthy of their brothers so that, at the time fixed by God, they will be able to contribute to the evangelization of the whole of China.

HELENE REICHL

AFRICA

Thanks to the assistance of the students of the African group at the International Center of Catechesis and the Pastorate, *Lumen Vitae,* we have been able to collect information on the catechumenate in Africa covering 16 dioceses in 12 different countries.[1] Their replies are samples enabling us to get a general idea of the situation. These students, who have personal experience of pastoral work in Africa, have for a long time in common reflected on the ideas of Vatican Council II concerning the restoration of the catechumenate; this enabled them to undertake an important pastoral investigation.

I

THE INSTITUTIONAL ASPECT

The Situation

The catechumenate appears to have been instituted everywhere in the Africa of the sub-Sahara, both in parishes and sub-parishes. For the greater part it depends on catechists. The diocesan statutes draw the attention of the clergy to the importance of this sector of the pastorate. In actual fact, only half of the replies show an interest that is truly deep; one third of the replies limit this interest to the final preparation made at the mission, while the rest show lack of interest. To what extent have nuns been consulted? It appears to be far too little; there are only six clearly positive replies on this subject. As for sponsorship, four replies show serious concern for this institution, two others note recent efforts to reappraise it, while the ten others admit that it is purely honorific. Is the Christian community involved with the catechumenate? Seven replies are positive, but in six cases it is only a question of apostolic activity to bring the pagans to the catechumenate. The seventh reply is very significant: because the baptismal rites have been divided into various stages, the

[1] For the West: Cameroons, Ghana, Mali, Nigeria. For Central Africa: Burundi, Congo-Léo, Rwanda. For the East: Tanzania, Uganda, Zambia. For the South: Rhodesia, Union of South Africa.

interest of the community of the faithful in the catechumens has been progressively aroused. A final aspect of the institution is the question of length: five replies mention four years, nine others speak of an official length of two years, but five of them state that this time is often reduced to one year and even to six months. One reply mentions a period of two to three months, while a final one states that the length of time is left to the discretion of the priest.

Pastoral Reflection

One can only rejoice in the fact that the institution of the catechumenate is solidly implanted in Africa. Historically, two tendencies have come together. The first inspired the pioneers of the modern missions and continued through three centuries. It depended on the theology of the time, ignoring for all practical purposes the great patristic tradition concerning the catechumenate. Worked out in a Christian world, it concerned itself almost exclusively with the baptism of babies. Moreover, influenced by the controversy with the Reformers, it insisted one-sidedly on the *ex opere operato* effect of the sacraments. Thus, it is understandable in these circumstances that missionaries are content with a very brief preparation which is intended to ensure the validity of the sacrament.

The second tendency was promoted by Cardinal Lavigerie. He initiated missions in the interior of the African continent and restored from the beginning the ancient practice of the catechumenate, requiring four years of preparation for baptism so that conversions would be real, genuine, informed and mature. This second tendency has finally imposed itself in the majority of African missions, although with some modifications, notably in the length of the catechumenate.[2]

The institution exists, but a serious pastoral effort must be undertaken in order to adapt it to the profound vision of the

[2] J. Beckmann, "L'Initiation et la célébration baptismale dans les Missions du 15e Siècle à nos jours," in *Maison-Dieu* 58 (1959), pp. 48-70. Cf. the original German text in *Neue Zeitschrift der Missionswissenschaft* 15 (1959).

mystery of the Church given to us by Vatican Council II. In particular, the catechumenate should be intimately integrated into the life of the parish: "The catechumenate should be taken care of not only by catechists or priests, but by the entire community of the faithful, especially by the sponsors." [3] At the moment the catechumenate appears a little like a marginal activity in the parish. When it was restored in central Africa it was not like this. The liturgical stages of baptism, celebrated with the active participation of the community of the faithful, will contribute to make the local Church aware of her maternal role in relation to the catechumens. In connection with the community of the faithful, the Council mentions godparents: with catechumens they will again exercise, in a more immediate fashion, the initiating function of the local Church, of which they ought to be considered delegates. The Council states that the role and the responsibility of the godparents will be more emphasized in the rites:[4] the restoration of the liturgy will thus furnish an important aid for the revaluing of sponsorship and, at the same time, be a very beneficial adaptation, because sponsorship is an integral part of animist religious initiations.

II

THE CATECHETICAL ASPECT

The Situation

All the replies agree that the catechumenate is organized in order to teach Christian doctrine and the customary prayers. The catechumens are sometimes divided into categories, each having a fixed study program: e.g., the great truths, dogma, morals and sacraments. Examinations determine the passage from one category to another. The individual contacts of the catechumens are primarily administrative in nature: interrogations and inquiries concerning their marital status.

An apostolic action, led primarily by the catechists and the

[3] *Decree on the Church's Missionary Activity* (n. 14).
[4] *The Constitution on the Sacred Liturgy* (n. 67).

militants of the lay movements, urges the pagans to join the catechumenate. The motive emphasized is "to serve God", and sometimes "to follow the way of the fathers", which requires some discussion of salvation. There are also other motives, notably human progress or family considerations. Once they have entered the catechumenate, the logic of the account of Christian truth is relied on, without scarcely bothering anymore about a formal evangelization, a pastorate of conversion or an authentic initiation.

Pastoral Reflection

In the face of this situation one can understand the insistence of the Council [5] that a true pastorate of evangelization, leading to Christian conversion, ought to precede the catechumenate proper. It consists in the proclamation of the living God and of Jesus Christ, sent by God for salvation. The living God is not merely the supreme being in whom the animists believe; it is God as he has revealed himself to man, intervening in the history of humanity, speaking to man, calling him to himself, making a covenant with him, sending his Son in order to achieve salvation by his death and his resurrection and sending his Spirit to all the faithful in order to make of them his children.

As for the catechumenate proper, according to the Council it ought to contain only those who are converted to Jesus Christ, in order to give them a Christian initiation. It is not a doctrinal system that should be given to them, but rather the vision, the very reality of the mystery of salvation to which God calls us to share in Christ. Thus, catechesis should be reorganized according to the perspectives of the history of salvation, and the catechumenate should make disciples of Christ of those who are converted. To this end a long contact with Christ as he is concretely presented in the synoptic gospels is absolutely indispensable. Moreover, they should have an apprenticeship in the life of the Church and the community of faith, of liturgy and of charity. Particular attention should be paid to the initiation into

[5] *Decree on the Church's Missionary Activity* (nn. 13, 14).

the liturgical signs which must be understood in the light of their scriptural equivalents. For such an initiation the time factor is very important. The length of the catechumenate should be determined according to the requirements of the end desired.

This reform of the catechumenate is basically only a return to the practice of the great missionaries who founded the Church in the heart of continental Africa. Father Lourdel of Uganda had an authentic pastorate of evangelization, announcing on every possible occasion the Good News of Jesus Christ. His catechumens became disciples of Christ, thanks to a long familiarity with St. Luke's gospel. In the martyrdom of Nyamugongo, they sealed this faith with their blood, this faith which had penetrated to the deepest levels of their personalities.

III

THE LITURGICAL ASPECT

The Situation

Out of sixteen replies to the inquiry, five give evidence of recent efforts to reestablish the liturgical stages of baptism. In four dioceses, the paschal vigil is kept as the normal date for the celebration of adult baptism. A general review of the organization of the catechumenate shows that it has developed independently of liturgical considerations. In fact, the solemn baptism of adults is conferred at very different dates, and sometimes fixed dates: three times a year (three replies), twice (seven replies), once (three replies), or else left to the discretion of the priest (three replies). As an immediate preparation, there is always a more intense period of instruction that is carried out in the parish, varying from two weeks to six months. A retreat of three or four days generally precedes baptism. Afterward the neophytes receive new instructions that are spread over a period of three days to six months in preparation for confirmation.

Pastoral Reflection

Taking account of previous legislation and of the ceremonial conception of the liturgy, it would be very wrong to blame missionaries for this situation. Whatever the recent past may have been, the conciliar directives urge that the liturgy be made the basis of the renewal of the catechumenate. The important things are: the restoration of the liturgical stages (notably in the rite of admission to the catechumenate and in the inscription in the category of the elect), Lent as a period of intense spiritual preparation for baptism (with scrutinies and other traditions), the connection between the sacraments and Christian initiation, their celebration during the paschal vigil, and, finally, the paschal period as a time of initiation of the neophytes into the realities of their regeneration, into the sacramental life and the mystery of the Church.

Thus, as with the other actions of the Church, the liturgy should become the summit and the source of the catechumenal pastorate. Appearing as a spiritual journey marked by a series of rites leading to the new birth in Christ, the catechumenate will fulfill the animists' profoundest aspirations, formulated in their religious initiations and made up of initiation rites marking the passage from an old to a new life.

In the missions, the full restoration of the catechumenate will undoubtedly prove the determining element in the renewal of the Church. Thanks to its vitality the community of the faithful will become aware that it is the baptismal community and the paschal community.

XAVIER SEUMOIS

VIETNAM

I was sent to make contact with a people that has not yet been evangelized: the Jörai, an ethnic minority in the central Plateau. This has enabled me to set up gradually a catechumenate that had not previously existed in this country. Subsequently the conciliar texts confirmed the importance of this personal initiative. My mission post became a catechumenate center for the Jörai, a diocesan service which continues to exist despite the state of war that has isolated me without any means of communication or information.

Almost all of the Jörai people have a traditional religion that actually makes it allergic to any other form of religion. Some Jörai, more or less civilized, live without religion. All are unaffected by verbal teaching and remarkably unstable in the practice (which for them is provisional) of all that is new and foreign to their customs.

Knowing this, one might easily conclude that pure preaching would be without effect and rapid "conversion" without any lasting fruit. But evangelization is not merely preaching, and a long catechumenate is able to make Christianity more than a "novelty". This is what my own particular situation suggested to me, and it resolved a difficulty which seemed to be discouraging.

"Make disciples of all nations . . ." (Mt. 28, 19-21). Evangelization—making disciples—means not only the Word to be heard, but also the Word to be nourished by. To evangelize is to liberate man's inner being, for the Word, which is the bread of life, is also the truth that makes us free. To evangelize is to place man within the mystery of this personal Word that is Christ— an incorporation that takes place progressively and begins with the entry into the catechumenate. To evangelize is not merely to touch individuals; it is to illuminate from within the genius of a people and to transform its structures. The catechumenate —the period of the conception of a new people—has a personal and a community dimension.

The Listeners

When one starts from nothing, one does not address Christians but primarily pagan "listeners". I first bear witness to my faith alone, and then together with catechumens as they come along. From the beginning each catechumen is a sign for all his pagan brothers, and later he becomes a sign in a special way for the one whom he brings to the gates of faith and whose godfather he then is.

Every Jörai is virtually a listener; however, strictly speaking, a listener is one who, without having the faith, is free to continue his pagan practices, and who agrees to have a prolonged contact with us, to come as a spectator to our assemblies, to which we admit him (except for the eucharistic liturgy). The entry into the catechumenate, a rogation procession and the blessing of the font are sacramental celebrations at which the presence of non-Christians is valuable. The listeners are also viewers. Jesus made gestures which were signs; we perform these signs again for our brothers. They are our rites (performed publicly and with a commentary) and also our own style of living the life of the people of this country.

This stage of being a listener, which links the world with the Church, is not to be neglected; it may last until all major obstacles to conversion have been removed.

The Entry into the Catechumenate

I have not encountered any unanimous group seeking conversion, nor am I able to admit an isolated individual. Experience has shown that he does not persevere. Whole families enter the catechumenate, the smallest unit that is viable in a pagan milieu.

The convert listener is brought by a responsible sponsor. His motives are examined by a council of sponsors. It is not possible to enter the catechumenate simply because one has followed courses of religious instruction or in order to marry a Christian; a man enters because he has started to believe. The postulant himself hands over the sacred objects which he possesses and declares that he is no longer bound by any vow or promise of sacrifice. He is then received ritually according to the Ordo of 1962, translated into Jörai.[1]

[1] My experience suggests that the monition of n. 4, which is abstruse and untranslatable, should be modified; that n. 42 (ingredere) should

Progress in Stages

Catechumens are educated individually by their sponsor and collectively by the liturgical assembly. Thus, not only is each stage celebrated liturgically, but the whole progressive initiation from stage to stage takes place within the framework of the liturgy and in connection with it.

The catechumens are judged by the Gospel in their lives (the interior illumination manifested by the *conversio morum*) and by their participation in the evangelization of their family (an influence shown by their good relations with pagans and by the listeners they bring along). There is no fixed time between the various stages. One moves from one stage to the next according to the signs that he gives of his transformation; the newly baptized have been in the catechumenate at least five years.

The catechumens pass through seven stages, celebrated during Lent at the beginning of the Mass of the catechumens. I use a system of pegs as a register, moving them according to the stages reached.

Problems

The *Constitution on the Sacred Liturgy* leaves it to the local ordinary to decide whether to introduce a catechumenate. The result is that one bishop does not dare to introduce it before other bishops in the same country, and that baptism, in practice, continues without any serious preparatory stages. I can testify that 99% of Jörai "baptized" in towns without a catechumenate abandon their religion once they have returned home.

The instability of the Jörai requires a long catechumenate. Some of them desire to remain catechumens all their lives, a problem that existed in the early Church. However, there are other problems in this long period. Married couples who are

---

have its place in the *primus gradus;* that in n. 9 (signing with the cross) a monition should inform the person that he is now becoming a Christian (*conceptus nondum natus*); that the *secundus gradus,* which is now of little significance, should be re-established, that there should be appropriate scriptural pericopes for each stage and that the rite should be placed within the Mass of the Catechumens (suppressing the final *Ite*).

catechumens may still beget children, and I am able neither to baptize these children nor to leave them as pagans. I cannot prevent young people from getting married, nor can I leave them without some marriage rite (if I did they would follow pagan rites, or would be considered and would consider themselves to be atheists). In both these cases I have had to improvise ceremonies, which are based on the blessings of the Ritual and also appeal to pagan cultural elements.[2]

The Jörai are developing and becoming civilized, and their traditional forms are being broken down. Catechumens slide toward atheism, and children born to parents who are catechumens do not always want to follow them. For this people, for whom liturgical action makes up the whole of religious activity, the liturgy, above all, can exercise a Christianizing influence. The fact is that our liturgy often has a de-Christianizing effect for its strangeness makes a man incapable of identifying himself with it. Thus, this meets the intimate and unavowed desire of all those who have come to the Church intending to pay only lip service and to use this stage in order to free themselves, progressively and without risk, from all religious life. Sincere in their intention of desacralizing an existence that has been alienated, they believe that Christianity will enable them to give themselves over freely to the activities of the world in order to develop like other peoples.

All this leads me to make further observations, to test, inquire and verify, in the fields of ethnography, sociology and psychology. Thus the catechumenate center tends to become more and more a center of missionary research, and perhaps that is what we ought to have had in the first place.

JACQUES DOURNES, M.E.P.

---

[2] For the initiation *per gradus,* properly speaking, it was not possible to adopt pagan ritual elements (cf. the *Constitution on the Sacred Liturgy,* n. 65). When I am able I prefer to do without these forms; if not I emphasize their provisional character. It is the permanent religious substratum of Jörai thinking, of the living man, that I am trying to take hold of and transform, rather than those forms which will soon be the folklore of the past.

BIOGRAPHICAL NOTES

HENDRIK MANDERS, C.SS.R.: Born in 1913 in Roosendall, Netherlands, he is a Redemptorist. He studied at the Angelicum in Rome and at the Sorbonne, gaining his doctorate in theology. A member of the Dutch Liturgical Commission, his works include *De liefde in de spiritualiteit van S. Alfonsus.*

LOUIS LIGIER, S.J.: Born in 1911 in Lons-le-Saunier, France, he was ordained in 1941. He studied at the Gregorian and gained his doctorate in theology. Since 1960 he has been professor of Oriental liturgy at the Oriental Institute in Rome. Among his works is *Péché d'Adam et péché du monde. Bible-Kippur Eucharistie* (2 vols.).

ALOIS STENZEL, S.J.: Born in 1917 in Schönheide, Germany, he was ordained in 1947, gaining his doctorate in theology in 1952. His publications include *Die Taufe. Eine genetische Erklärung der taufliturgie.*

MICHEL DUJARIER: Born in 1932 in Tours, he studied at the Gregorian and at the Catholic Institute in Paris, gaining his doctorate in theology in 1961. A priest "Fidei Donum" in Dahomey, he contributes to *La Maison-Dieu.*

THIERRY MAERTENS, O.S.B.: Born in 1921 in Huy, Belgium, he was ordained in 1946. He is the editor of *Paroisse et Liturgie* and *Année de pastorale liturgique* and the author of numerous articles on the liturgy.

ROGER BÉRAUDY, S.S.: Born in 1925 in Ambert, France, he was ordained as a Sulpician in 1948. He studied at the Catholic University of Lyons and became a doctor of theology in 1953. He is now superior of the university seminary at Lyons. His works include *Les catégories de pensée de Ratramne dans son enseignement eucharistique.*

EMIL LENGELING: Born in 1916 in Dortmund, he was ordained in 1941. He studied at the Universities of Rome and Munich, gaining his doctorate in theology in 1947. A professor of liturgy at Münster University, he has authored numerous articles on the liturgy.

JOSEPH GELINEAU, S.J.: Born in 1929 in Lyons, he was ordained in 1951. He studied at the Catholic Institute in Paris, gaining his doctorate in theology in 1960. A professor of pastoral liturgy, his works include *Voices and Instruments in Christian Worship.*

CHARLES PALIARD: Born in 1929 in Lyons, he was ordained in 1957. He studied in Lyons and at L'Institut supérieur catéchétique in Paris. He is an assistant director of religious education in Lyons.

WILHELM BREUNING: Born in 1920 in Sobernheim, Germany, he was ordained in 1948. He studied at the Universities of Trèves and Bonn, gaining his doctorate in theology in 1954. A professor of dogmatic theology at Trèves University, his works include *Die hypostatische Union in der Theologie Wilhelms von Auxerre, Hugos von St. Cher u. Roland von Cremona.*

LUCIANO BORELLO, S.D.B.: Born in 1927 in Mango, Italy, he was ordained as a Salesian in 1956. A doctor of philosophy and theology, he is a member of the editorial committee of the review *Catechesi.* His works include *La Santa Messa azione sacra della communita.*

DOMINGO COLS: Born in 1928 in San Pablo de Ordal, Spain, he was ordained in 1952. He is choirmaster of Barcelona Cathedral and a consultant to the Episcopal Commission on the Liturgy.

STEPHEN SOMERVILLE: Born in 1931 in London, he was ordained in 1956. He is a member of the International Commission for English in the Liturgy and he teaches liturgy at St. Michael's Choir School in Quebec.

MOIRA KEARNEY: Born in 1917 in Durban, she is an organist, choirmistress and composer of liturgical music.

AMARO CAVALCANTI DE ALBUQUERQUE: Born in 1928 in Juiz de Fora, Brazil, he was ordained in 1955. He is a professor of sacred music and president of the National Brazilian Commission for Sacred Music.

REINHARD KÖSTERS: Born in 1931 in Delbrück, Germany, he was ordained in 1958. He received his doctorate in theology from Innsbruck University in 1965 and now has his own parish.

BERNARD GUILLARD: Born in 1921 in Nantes, he was ordained in 1945. He is the director of the National Catechumenate Office.

IGNACIO OÑATIBIA: Born in 1918 in Oyarzun, Spain, he was ordained in 1941. He studied at Catholic University in Washington, gained his doctorate in theology and now teaches dogmatic theology and liturgy. Among his publications is *Los Sacramentos et el Misterio Pascual.*

JAIRO MEJÍA GOMEZ: Born in 1922 in Aguadas, Colombia, he was ordained in 1945. An advisor to the post-conciliar Liturgical Commission, his publications include *Directorio Liturgico.*

FRANCIS TSUCHIYA, S.J.: Born in 1926 in Tokyo, he was ordained in 1958, gaining doctorates in philosophy in 1954 and theology in 1959. He is a professor of theology at Sophia University in Tokyo and secretary of the Japanese Liturgical Commission.

HELENE REICHL: Born in 1934, she is the head of the Center for Catechetical and Social Training "Fons Vitae" in Taipei, Formosa.

XAVIER SEUMOIS: Born in 1915 in Jemeppe, Belgium, he was ordained in 1939. He is director of the African Catechetical Institute.

JACQUES DOURNES, M.E.P.: Born in 1922 in Saint-Pol, France, he joined the Foreign Missionary Society of Paris and was ordained in 1945. He is presently a missionary in Vietnam. His publications include *Dieu aime les païens*.

International Publishers of CONCILIUM

ENGLISH EDITION
Paulist Press
Glen Rock, N. J., U.S.A.

Burns & Oates Ltd.
25 Ashley Place
London, S.W.1

DUTCH EDITION
Uitgeverij Paul Brand, N. V.
Hilversum, Netherlands

FRENCH EDITION
Maison Mame
Tours/Paris, France

GERMAN EDITION
Verlagsanstalt Benziger & Co., A.G.
Einsiedeln, Switzerland

Matthias Grunewald-Verlag
Mainz, W. Germany

SPANISH EDITION
Ediciones Guadarrama
Madrid, Spain

PORTUGUESE EDITION
Livraria Morais Editora, Ltda.
Lisbon, Portugal

ITALIAN EDITION
Editrice Queriniana
Brescia, Italy